Gardens of Great Britain & Ireland

YOUR GUIDE TO 100 OF THE MOST BEAUTIFUL GARDENS

CONTENTS

Wales 138

Scotland 158

Ireland 196

Clockwise from top left
The Water Garden at Beth Chatto Gardens in the East of England (see page 62).

Geranium 'Mount Venus' abounds at Hunting Brook Gardens in the Republic of Ireland (see page 216).

Mountains provide the magnificent backdrop for Plas Brondanw in Wales (see page 144).

Introduction

The inhabitants of Great Britain and Ireland have, for many centuries, created gardens for many purposes. At first, all gardens were an extension of farms. People grew food to keep themselves and their families alive – their lives were preoccupied by the need simply to subsist, with not a lot of time for the pure pleasure of gardening. Who knows who first thought of the idea of just enjoying a garden? I like to think it was a monk who rose early to tend the monastic vegetable garden. That morning, as the sun was pressing through a gauzy mist, he noticed a lone flowering plant that was neither edible nor useful but was just there. It made him smile so he allowed it to stay, and the notion of a pleasure garden was born. Bit cheesy? Probably, but you get my drift.

From that moment on there has been a (slightly staccato) journey to the gardens showcased in this fine book. We have gone through medieval bowers, Tudor herbals, 18th-century landscape gardens, the great Victorian plant-hunting era, and on to the first naturalistically planted gardens in the early 1900s. The construction of suburbs and new towns has given more garden space to everyone (not just the rich), and today there is a welcome rise in the idea of gardening in harmony with the natural world rather than fighting against it with controls and chemicals. Above all, the making of gardens requires two things: peace and prosperity. If a country is unsettled during times of war, gardens revert to being places to grow food – for example, the Dig for Victory campaign during the Second World War – because we first need to feed our bodies before we can feed our souls.

Gardens are one of those things the people of Britain and Ireland are very good at (along with sponge cakes, new music, and the invention of cricket). Many other people were gardening earlier: the Chinese, for example, were making highly sophisticated gardens in the 11th century BCE, at which point Britons were still bashing

each other over the head with stone clubs. The Hanging Gardens of Babylon and Japanese temple gardens got in there earlier too, but, as is evident from the huge range of gardens in this book, we have managed to catch up.

The geography of Britain and Ireland offered a head start, furnishing a perfect gardening climate, with even temperatures and the sort of weather that makes gardens glow and plants flourish. We shall gloss over the flaws in this theory: too much rain, not enough rain, too much sun, not enough sun, and, of course, the omnipresence of slugs. These islands also have the advantage of many microclimates, from the warm, wet West of Ireland (where ferns grow as tall as houses) to the rocky fringes of the Pennines. This is mostly sheer luck, as most of us have ended up here through the vagaries of fate and the decisions of our ancestors. However, for the actual creation and continued maintenance of our gardens, the British and Irish can take much more credit.

Remember my fantasy monk and the idea of a garden making you smile? All of the gardens in this book serve that purpose in one way or another; whether they embrace acreages or tiny urban corners, they are all guaranteed to make you feel better. Some gardens induce a sense of relaxation and peace, some excite or energize, while others educate. It is something of a cliché, but there really is something for everyone in these gardens – from the horti-fanatic eager to discover new plants and styles, to the smallest child whose only interest is running around exploring everything until they finally collapse into the comforting arms of a large piece of cake. We also have the massive advantage of three well-established gardening charities, the Royal Horticultural Society (RHS), the National Trust, and the Royal Horticultural Society of Ireland (RHSI), which not only open their own gardens to the public, but are also there to make the process of gardening easier, by advancing horticultural knowledge.

Far left *Garden views stretch across Loch Carron to the Isle of Skye at Attadale in the Scottish Highlands (see page 162).*

Centre *Drought-tolerant plants thrive in RHS Hyde Hall's Dry Garden in Essex (see page 64).*

Left *A masterclass in naturalistic planting at June Blake's Garden in the Republic of Ireland (see page 220).*

Some of these gardens are classic choices with sweeping lawns and rose gardens. There are examples from the great 18-century golden age (including a few touched by Lancelot "Capability" Brown, who created more than 170 gardens during his illustrious career as a landscape architect), but there are lots of other examples that have been created (or updated) more recently, from unexpected corners of busy cities, to gardens designed by artists, and empty fields converted into plant heaven.

There are gardens here from right across all the nations and regions, and you should use the book as an excuse to range far and wide. Gardens change depending on the region: for example, the gardens of the South West of England are not the same as the gardens of Scotland. There are the obvious differences in growing conditions, but it is also a matter of regional style. Irish gardens, especially the more recently established, tend to be exuberant and colourful, and inject a touch of Irish iconoclasm into the old, pre-Independence Victorian formality, while many Scottish gardens have very close connections with the surrounding landscape. The South of England and Wicklow County in Ireland probably offer the greatest choice, but there are gems to be unearthed from Anglesey to Mull. The seaside is not just for beaches, nor are mountains just for climbing – they also have gardens to visit.

When gardeners are not gardening they are usually at their happiest doing one of three things: shopping (for new plants), visiting gardens (in search of inspiration and ideas to borrow), or, especially in the colder months or on rainy days, reading magazines, books, or websites so they can find out everything they can about gardens. If they can do all three at once, they will be in heaven – that's where this book can help.

James Alexander-Sinclair

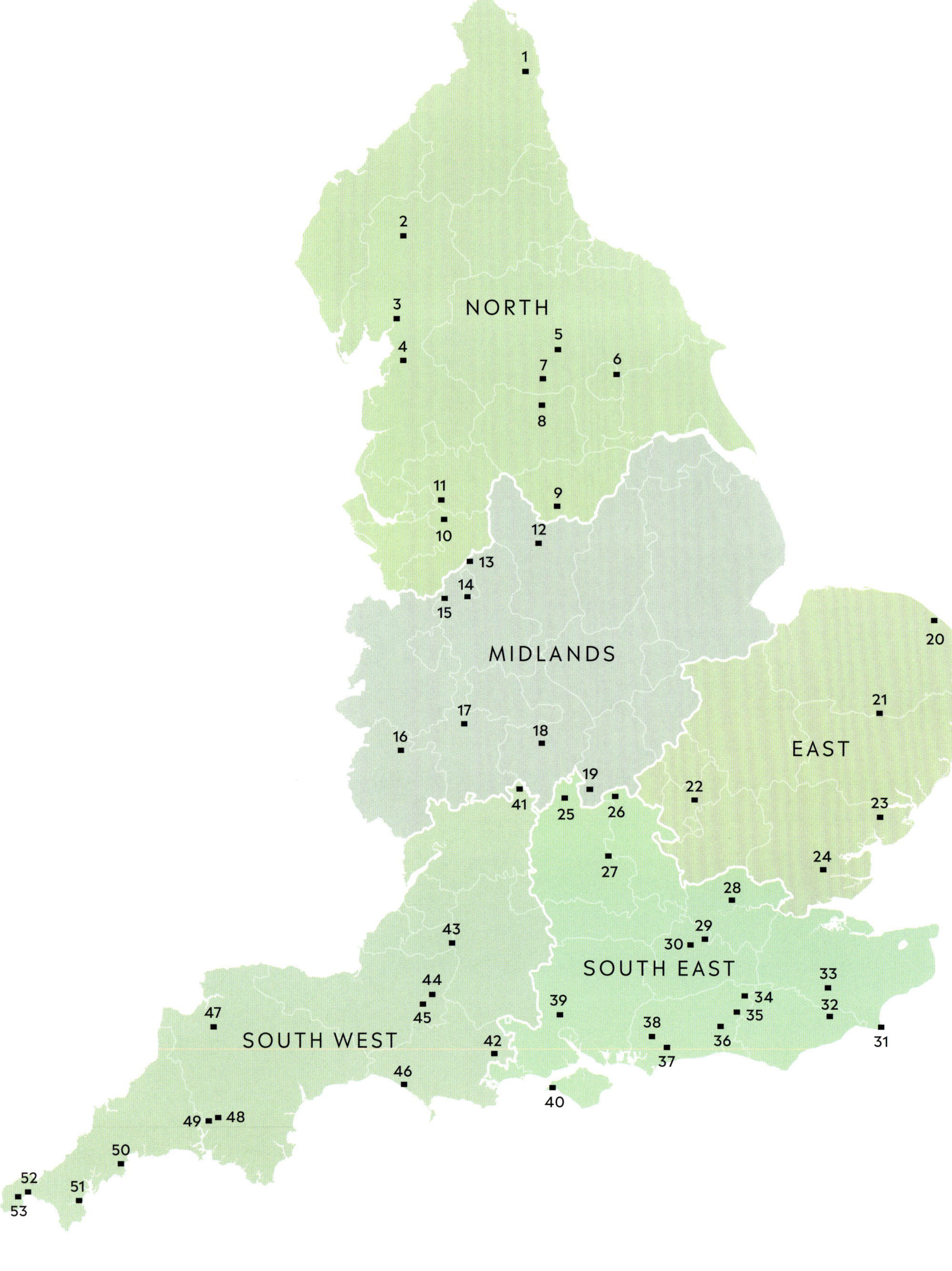

NORTH
MIDLANDS
EAST
SOUTH EAST
SOUTH WEST
1
2
3
4
5
6
7
8
9
10
11
12
13
14
15
16
17
18
19
20
21
22
23
24
25
26
27
28
29
30
31
32
33
34
35
36
37
38
39
40
41
42
43
44
45
46
47
48
49
50
51
52
53
54

England

No one garden can truly capture the essence of English gardens, such is their diversity and individuality. Here you will discover subtropical coastal gardens, picturesque parklands, bountiful walled gardens, fragrant rose gardens, dazzling herbaceous borders, and sculptural topiary gardens, which, collectively, demonstrate just what makes an English garden.

Home to 329 'Taihaku' cultivars, Alnwick's cherry orchard is the largest outside Japan and breathtaking in bloom.

The Alnwick Garden

WHERE *Alnwick, Northumberland, NE66 1YU* WHEN *Open all year except January; at its best in spring for blossom or summer for roses* WHAT *An adventure playground of a garden in the grounds of historic Alnwick Castle*

Alnwick can claim to be one of the most ambitious new gardens of the twenty-first century thanks to the vision of Jane, the Duchess of Northumberland. It is a fully immersive experience for the whole family.

The second-largest inhabited castle in the UK, Alnwick has been the seat of the Percy family for 700 years. The garden has been dramatically developed over the last 25 years by Jane Percy, and is now far removed from the original concept that was created in 1750.

On arrival, it is the iconic Grand Cascade that grabs the attention. Set on a steep hillside, it is unmissable, and the 120 erupting water jets make this impressive feature the ever-changing and dramatic heart of the garden.

NEXT GENERATION

Within the huge expanse of garden there's further adventure to be found for the whole family. The experience that children gain from the garden has been the Percy family's focus, and they encourage them to freely enjoy the space. The new play area, the fantastical world of Lilidorei, is dedicated to children, though this in no way weakens the horticultural prowess and innovation of the garden.

Alnwick offers a raft of garden spaces that are both beautiful and intriguing. With over 3,000 roses flowering in June and July, the Rose Garden is a gallery of scented blooms, and features its own soft-pink species, 'The Alnwick Rose'. The Poison Garden, meanwhile, which remains locked and is only accessible on guided tours, is home to deadly plants – with every tour comes a wealth of gory stories.

At the top of the hill the Ornamental Garden makes the walk worthwhile. It was once the kitchen garden and is now designed as a series of "rooms", where you will find an impressive 16,000 European plants. At the centre is a pool that feeds into shallow rills, while the garden is surrounded by a pergola dressed with climbers, ensuring head-to-toe interest.

Water plays a large part in Alnwick's offering, with the Serpent Garden – so-called due to the coils of topiary that snake their way throughout – featuring eight water sculptures by William Pye. It's clear that sensation and stimulation are key throughout Alnwick, whether that's the sound of water, the sight of beautiful blossom in spring, or getting lost in the towering *Fargesia rufa* of the Bamboo Labyrinth. This whole garden is as much about people as it is about plants, and guarantees an immersive experience.

Lowther Castle Gardens

WHERE *Penrith, Cumbria, CA10 2HH* WHEN *Year-round interest; the Rose Garden, parterre, and herbaceous borders are at their best in summer* WHAT *A unique and romantic garden created in the past 20 years around and within the castle ruins*

Lowther Castle was built on the site of an earlier house, in the early nineteenth century, for the 1st Earl of Lonsdale. Less than 130 years later that palatial mansion was abandoned and left to become a ruin. Today, however, nature is reclaiming its crumbling walls.

Thanks to a penchant for yellow Rolls-Royces, the 5th Earl of Lonsdale racked up huge debts, so when he died in 1944, Lowther Castle's contents were sold off, the roof removed, a pig farm put inside, chicken sheds erected across the gardens, and the rest of the 49-hectare (120-acre) estate covered with Sitka spruce.

In 2006, current custodian William James Lowther (known as Jim) decided to repurpose the castle as a truly magnificent backdrop for a new garden and, with the help of designer Dan Pearson, the project commenced in 2008.

The result is undoubtedly a tour de force, but also one of the most unique garden creations of the twenty-first century. For, not only does it surround the castle; it actually runs through the very heart of the old building.

NATURE HEALS

The crumbling walls call to mind the atmospheric remains of Tintern or Fountains Abbey. In the eighteenth century, their eroding Gothic arches were softened by clambering ivy, so beloved by the Romantics. At Lowther, Dan Pearson has chosen climbing roses, clematis, *Akebia longeracemosa*, and *Vitis coignetiae* to clothe the wounded walls, yet the metaphor for the healing power of nature is just as potent.

To the front of the ruined castle, a newly planted yew parterre brims with tapestries of perennials, such as *Stachys byzantina*, *Salvia pratensis* 'Indigo', and *Potentilla nepalensis* 'Miss Willmott'. Each is cleverly planted with grasses, which sway rhythmically in the breezes issuing from nearby Lowther Valley and the Lake District fells beyond. In contrast (and this garden is all about contrasts: old and new; ruination and regeneration; soft plantings and hard architecture), a series of clipped hornbeams in the nearby restored Courtyard stand rigidly to attention, their sculpted shapes reflecting the castle's skyline of towers and buttresses.

Jim has also ventured into the wider landscape, clearing Sitka spruce as he goes, while restoring original features, such as the Edwardian Rock Garden and Japanese Garden, as well as creating modern features, including a new Rose Garden and Orchard.

In England over the past 50 years there have been garden restorations aplenty, but none quite like Lowther. Here, a vibrant new place is reinventing itself on the bones of the past.

Top *The Parterre, by Dan Pearson, where* Filipendula, Veronicastrum, *and* Salvia *soften the castle ruins.*

Bottom *The clipped hornbeams look strikingly modern against the historic Courtyard.*

FOCUS ON

Then and Now

Lowther's original gardens were laid out in the seventeenth century. A great yew avenue was complemented by knot gardens where fruit and vegetables were grown for the previous hall's kitchens. Garden relics such as the Roman bath and ornamental stone columns are reminders of Lowther's Victorian Garden, while the restored Iris Gardens date from the Edwardian period when renowned designer Thomas Mawson was commissioned to work on the garden.

Top *Even in mid-winter the ancient topiary brings magical structure and character to Levens Hall.*

Bottom *Hot pinks and rich purples dance in the colour-themed herbaceous borders in high summer.*

Levens Hall

WHERE *Kendal, Cumbria, LA8 0PD* WHEN *March to October for superb topiary; summer for herbaceous borders* WHAT *A historical Grade I-listed garden dating from 1694, famous for its ancient and magnificent topiary*

Levens Hall boasts some of the oldest topiary in the world. The garden was originally laid out in 1694 by the former King James II's gardener, Frenchman Guillaume Beaumont, who had trained under André Le Nôtre at Versailles and then worked on the grounds of Hampton Court Palace. His creations remain, as beautiful and fantastical as ever.

Perhaps the two most surprising things about Levens Hall are how Beaumont was enticed from royal palaces to a comparatively humble manor house in Westmorland (now Cumbria), and how its remarkable garden has survived pretty much intact for over 300 years.

The first question is relatively easy to answer. Levens Hall was purchased in the late 1680s by Colonel James Grahme (or Graham), previously keeper of the privy purse to James II, who had witnessed Beaumont's skill first-hand at Hampton Court. Not only was Grahme well connected, but he also had money to spend.

The garden's survival can be summed up by the fact that it has had only ten head gardeners in its 300-year existence. Couple this continuity with periods of owner poverty and inertia, and you can see how the years may have rolled by with little change. That is, other than the size of Beaumont's abstract and geometric yew and box topiary shapes – over 100 of them in all – which have grown to gargantuan proportions, some now in excess of 9 metres (30ft) tall.

To stand among these gloriously flamboyant evergreen chess pieces, giant mushrooms, coronets, domes, lions, statuesque peacocks, and even beer jugs is without doubt one of England's horticultural highlights and one that should be experienced at least once.

CONTINUITY AND CHANGE

Topiary, however, is only part of the Levens story. It is now the beloved home of the Bagot family, who in 1994, to celebrate the tercentenary of the Grahme and Beaumont partnership, designed a delightful new Fountain Garden bordered with pleached limes.

They, along with their head gardener of 30 years, Chris Crowder, also began to plant bulbs such as tulips and sweeping summer carpets of antirrhinum, lavender, and verbena around the topiary. So successful were these colourful additions that they now annually grow on-site more than 30,000 bedding plants. Rose gardens, wildflower meadows, bee borders, and magnificent pastel-shaded and hot-coloured herbaceous borders add yet more to the mix, ensuring that Levens is no longer a garden set in time, but a dynamic, everchanging landscape of colour, form, and texture.

Gresgarth Hall

WHERE *Caton, Lancaster, Lancashire, LA2 9NB* WHEN *All year; particularly late spring for candelabra primulas and rhododendrons* WHAT *A private garden of exceptional design in an immersive romantic setting*

Home of the celebrated landscape designer Arabella Lennox-Boyd and her husband Mark since the late 1970s, Gresgarth Hall is the place to discover thousands of rare trees and shrubs. The result is a garden with magical year-round interest.

What was neglected land when the Lennox-Boyds arrived has been transformed over the last 40 years by Arabella into a work of art that demonstrates both masterful plant selection and thoughtful design. Gresgarth has been in experienced hands, as her career has seen her design six RHS gold-medal-winning Chelsea Flower Show gardens, and hundreds of others worldwide.

Arabella grew up in Italy in a house at the top of a hill, so she took time to get acquainted with the very different challenges of a Lancashire garden at the foot of a hill, where acid soil, rain, and wind were all dominating factors. Trees were cut down and views opened from the house across to the river to make way for a garden that is home to many thoughtful touches – for example, the intricately designed stone mosaic walkways.

A NATURAL BLEND

This near-5-hectare (12-acre) garden has all the ingredients you could desire, with a Wild Garden, Rhododendron Woodland, Vegetable Garden, impressive collection of trees and shrubs, herbaceous borders, and a lake and pond. The rushing water of the Artle Beck that travels through the garden adds a sense of drama and provides the mood music to any visit.

The garden unfolds from the Gothic-style house, starting with formal terraces where evergreen topiary hedges frame the more relaxed style beyond. Here, the drama of the house is doubled thanks to the reflection in the pond. Arabella's considered design has allowed the formal areas of the garden to merge with the more natural areas over the river, so that the garden fits like a glove into the landscape.

The garden is home to collections of magnolias, acers, rhododendrons, and a National Collection of *Styracaceae*. The mature trees and shrubs ensure interest all year and are planted so as to make this garden a real joy to explore. The more architectural shapes of the topiary take over in the winter.

Evidence of Arabella's colour crafting can be seen in the double herbaceous borders in summer, which are backed by formal yew hedging and feature blooms of pink, blue, burgundy, and white. They demonstrate that Gresgarth is the epitome of a romantic garden, thanks to decades of judicious curation.

Top *Blue camassias in May contrast beautifully with lime-green euphorbia.*

Bottom *The Vegetable Garden is home to dahlias and sweet peas, as well as fruit and vegetables.*

GARDEN INSPIRATION

Raising Vegetables

The sloping, north-facing Kitchen Garden offers a lesson in planting edibles for taste as well as decoration. Crops have been planted in stepped terraces and in raised beds so that rich soil could be incorporated. Although a large, productive garden, it shows what can be grown on a smaller scale, even with the darkest aspect and poor soil.

Newby Hall's National Collection of Cornus (flowering dogwoods) has over 100 specimens, which bloom in May and June.

Newby Hall Gardens

WHERE *Ripon, North Yorkshire, HG4 5AE* WHEN *Late spring for primulas; summer for the herbaceous borders and Rose Garden* WHAT *Award-winning gardens, mostly created in the early 1920s, surrounding a seventeenth-century house*

Newby Hall's present 16-hectare (40-acre) garden is mostly the work of Major Edward Compton, who inherited the estate in 1921. Although he was greatly influenced by his friend Captain Lawrence Johnston of Hidcote Manor in Gloucestershire (see page 104), Compton's garden at Newby Hall has its own enchanting character.

When Major Compton inherited the stunning Grade I-listed Newby Hall, built between 1691 and 1695 to a Christopher Wren design, there was little remaining of the formal Dutch-style gardens laid out by original head gardener Peter Aram, other than the Lime Avenue to the west of the current garden. Compton, in turn, swept away most of the ostentatious Victorian features that had been overlaid on Aram's design, planting hedges and trees to protect the new garden from the biting Yorkshire winds. He then created a main-axis grass walkway through the garden, sloping down from the house to the River Ure.

Either side of this he planted a pair of deep herbaceous borders 200 metres (656ft) long, backed by crisp, closely clipped yew hedges. One hundred years later, these magnificent borders are perhaps Newby's best-known feature, planted with a range of herbaceous perennials, which ensure colour and interest throughout the main season. They are undoubtedly part of the reason why in 2019 Newby received the prestigious Historic Houses Garden of the Year Award.

LASTNG LEGACY

Behind the borders is a series of 14 garden rooms, each with a different theme, colour scheme, or planting style, which make any visit to Newby a delightful journey of discovery.

Elsewhere there is much more to enjoy. The Rose Garden features a scented profusion of old-fashioned blooms, including damask, centifolia, and alba. In the stepped Water Garden you'll find a wonderful collection of RHS Harlow Carr candelabra primulas (see page 24), at their best in late May and June, while in the Tropical Garden yuccas, eryngiums, and *Eucalyptus gunnii* push the boundaries of what can be grown this far north. In the relaxed Orchard Garden quince and apple trees are underplanted with long grass dotted with tulips and fritillaria in spring, while the Woodland Garden, partly attributed to Edwardian designer Ellen Willmott, contains a number of original introductions of plant hunter Ernest Wilson.

Compton died in 1977, having spent over 50 years creating this remarkable garden, but its care remains with the Compton family, who continue to honour his legacy.

Breezy Knees

WHERE *Common Lane, Warthill, York, YO19 5XS* WHEN *From May until September; spring for irises and peonies; summer for flower meadows, roses, and herbaceous borders* WHAT *A beautiful modern garden created on a barefield site over the past 25 years*

In 1998, pharmacist Colin Parker and his wife Marylen decided to give up the day jobs and (with no previous horticultural training) create a garden from scratch. They purchased an 8-hectare (20-acre) parcel of arable farmland, with no accompanying house, from the local council and in 1999 first put their spades into the ground.

The site had wonderful views towards York Minster, but no protection from the often-biting winds that sweep across the Vale of York, which inspired the garden's name: Breezy Knees. To rectify this, the Parkers spent the first eight years simply planting trees and shrubs to bring structure and shelter to the exposed site.

It hasn't all been plain sailing since, however. In the winter of 2010 temperatures dipped to -19°C (66°F), killing off some plantings. It was a hard but valuable lesson for the couple, who since then have ensured that whatever they plant can survive the coldest Yorkshire winters.

Some of the early plantings that survived are now over 16 metres (50ft) tall and provide focal points as well as structure and shelter. Today, the garden extends to 10 hectares (25 acres) and contains over 7,000 plant varieties, making it one of the largest "new" gardens in Yorkshire.

THEMED DISPLAYS

The garden is arranged into a series of diverse areas, each with a different theme. Colin and Marylen have created monthly borders, which display flowers blooming at their best in each month. For instance, in the May Garden there are stunning collections of irises and peonies, which also add vibrant splashes of colour to the Pond and Shade Gardens. In June and July, it is the Rock Garden's turn to take centre stage, along with wonderful collections of daylilies (*Hemerocallis*).

By midsummer these give way to the annual flower meadow, and the Cottage Garden, with its relaxed, tumbling feel and muted pastel shades. On warm days the air in the Rose Garden is full of intoxicating fragrances. Meandering "rivers" of achillea lead the garden into August, along with the main herbaceous border, which remains a riot of colour until the fading embers of late September.

Nothing ever stands still here. Every year the Parkers add new plants, redesign borders, and generally improve the garden. Yet sweeping lawns, conifers, ornamental grasses, fountains, and water features slow the tempo and allow enough breathing space for visitors to revel in the peace and tranquillity to be found here.

Clockwise from top *Heleniums, eryngiums, and betony create contrast in the summer borders.*

Giant Wellingtons add a playful touch.

*Globe thistles (*Echinops*) bring striking drama and form to the borders.*

GARDEN INSPIRATION

A Sense of Fun

Colin and Marylen both have a sense of fun, so Breezy Knees is full of quirky surprises. There's a large topiary creation called Stonehedge, which is a hornbeam version of Stonehenge in Wiltshire. Overlooking the Rose Garden are two gigantic, sculptured Wellington boots, and there is even a Rogues' Gallery border, full of thuggish plants that traditionally run amok but gardeners love to hate.

The Sandstone Rock Garden glows in autumn as evergreen trees and shrubs set off the array of vibrant Japanese maples.

RHS Garden Harlow Carr

WHERE *Harrogate, North Yorkshire, HG3 1QB* WHEN *All year round*
WHAT *A varied garden set in a shallow valley with naturalistic streamside plantings, expansive Rock Garden, and Winter Walk*

The cool, moist conditions enjoyed at RHS Garden Harlow Carr allow a dazzling range of plant collections to flourish, from waterside primulas to rare alpine species. With its diverse features and planting styles, this is a garden for everyone, at any time of year.

The story of Harlow Carr – today one of the UK's leading gardens – begins in the nineteenth century when the site was home to a bathhouse and hotel, its grounds featuring natural springs providing health-giving spa water. In the 1950s the Northern Horticultural Society (NHS) leased the land to create new trial gardens testing the hardiness and suitability of plants for the northern climate. In 2001 the NHS merged with the Royal Horticultural Society and a new phase of development began.

Historic features such as the Bath House and redeveloped Harrogate Arms Café lend the garden an appealing suggestion of age. The Sandstone Rock Garden, installed in the 1950s, has been refurbished with a collection of Japanese maples and dwarf pines, while the original Main Borders were replanted in 2004 with a prairie-style blend of perennials and grasses. They have recently been refreshed with a focus on late-season interest, with paths that weave through the beds and make the planting more immersive. Woodland (a remnant of the ancient Forest of Knaresborough) covers half the garden – most trees are natives, although an understorey of rhododendrons was planted in the 1950s. A long-term project to restore overgrown woodland areas includes a rhododendron propagation project, focusing on the most vulnerable species. Recent planting has added choice ornamentals to the Woodland such as summer-flowering *Stewartia* and *Clethra*.

SOMETHING FOR EVERYONE

One of the key characteristics of Harlow Carr is its diversity. The fine Kitchen Garden grows produce for the café. The vivid Sub-Tropicana Garden, with its exotic plantings, and the

Clockwise from top left *This area by the Kitchen Garden is alive in spring with masses of flowering daffodil bulbs.*

Flaming cornus stems in the Winter Walk ensure vibrant colour even during the coldest months.

Rudbeckia, perovskia, and helenium combine with grasses to create the prairie-style Main Borders.

Mediterranean-inspired Sun Border push the boundaries of what plants can be grown in Yorkshire, while alpines have long been a speciality. As well as the Alpine House, where *Lewisia*, *Dionysia*, *Sempervivum*, and others are grown to perfection, outside is the newly created alpine rockery made from repurposed local limestone. This provides both a showcase for the plants and an outdoor laboratory to study their response to climate change.

Perhaps the best-known area at Harlow Carr is Streamside, which runs through the heart of the site. In early summer the banks of the burn dazzle with wonderful displays from a swarm of candelabra *Primula* Harlow Car (sic) hybrids, which sparkle in a mix of bright colours.

The moist, cool conditions suit other exciting plants, too, including *Meconopsis*, *Hosta*, and *Iris sibirica*. In recent years plantings of *Cornus*, new bridges, dry-stone walls, and terracing have been added to help protect against floodwater erosion. The Queen Mother's Lake offers more waterside planting, plus abundant wildlife.

Even in winter there is much to see. The heather beds by the entrance create bold drifts of colour from January to March. And don't miss the Winter Walk, which winds through beds of fiery *Cornus*, snow-white *Betula*, sweet-scented daphne, and early bulbs such as *Galanthus*, *Iris reticulata*, and *Cyclamen coum* – all combined with panache.

FOCUS ON

Geoffrey Smith

A well-known writer and presenter of the BBC's *Gardeners' World*, Geoffrey Smith (1928–2009) was also responsible for much of the early development of Harlow Carr, serving as superintendent until 1974. He experimented with growing plants once considered unsuitable for northern gardens, and developed the Arboretum and Streamside area, where today a memorial stone to him lies.

TIMELINE OF EVENTS

1949

Land leased by the Northern Horticultural Society (NHS) to make a garden at Harlow Carr.

1950

Harlow Carr first opens to the public.

1954

Geoffrey Smith becomes garden superintendent.

1960s

Streamside and Woodland areas are developed.

1970s

The garden grows from 10.5 to 27.5 hectares (26 to 68 acres).

2004

The Main Borders are replanted.

2009

The Alpine House is completed.

2010

The Bramall Learning Centre and Teaching Garden opens.

2020

The Sub-Tropicana Garden is developed.

2021

The Thaliana Bridge opens over the Queen Mother's Lake.

York Gate

WHERE *Adel, Leeds, LS16 8DW* WHEN *All year round for interest in the garden rooms, structure, and details in the hard landscaping* WHAT *An Arts and Crafts garden with exceptional elements of garden design*

This magical Grade II-listed garden is influenced by the Arts and Crafts movement, which advocated traditional craftsmanship and combining the formal and informal. Inspiring plant combinations, meticulous details, and exquisite garden rooms make it a must-visit.

York Gate was created from farmland by Frederick Spencer, his wife Sybil, and their son Robin between 1951 and 1994. In its use of garden rooms, handcrafted architectural details, and structural topiary mixed with informal planting, it translates the features of an Arts and Crafts garden into a style that integrates perfectly into its 0.4-hectare (1-acre) plot, creating a masterpiece of garden design.

EYE-CATCHING DETAILS

The garden is divided into 14 rooms by trimmed beech and yew hedges that frame a succession of paths, vistas, and focal points. Quirky topiary draws attention throughout, particularly the row of yew sails near the house, and the spirals that set off the beautiful Herb Garden, which bursts with alliums as well as edibles in spring.

The small Tropical Garden is packed with fuchsias, tree ferns, scheffleras, and other leafy exotics. A greenhouse and stone terrace provide a perfect home for tiny jewel-like alpines and succulents, while a hay meadow – habitat for orchids, fritillaries, and a host of other wildflowers – supplies local farmers with livestock feed.

TRADITION REIMAGINED

Beautifully crafted architectural structures in natural materials, such as the Folly, the Arbour, and the Tall Sundial, also catch the eye in autumn and winter when the bones of the garden become prominent. It then bursts into life in spring with tulips, followed by burgeoning borders. Don't miss the espaliered cedar and pyracanthas climbing up the side of the house.

Although little of the original design has changed, the palette has expanded to create multi-layered plantings, introducing more modern combinations to the traditional structure. Blue Himalayan poppies sit among the ferns in the Dell, for example, and sword-like *Astelia chathamica* next to white-flowered foxgloves and astrantia of the White Garden.

The hard landscaping, which is also outstanding, adds artisanal charm throughout. This includes stone setts laid as a circular maze in the gravel, spiralling around a reclaimed millstone, as well as a diamond-patterned path leading to a small gazebo – all testament to the Spencers' dedication to gardening and garden design as both an art and a craft.

"It was in the garden where my heart lay."

ROBIN SPENCER

Top *Myriad textures and tones form the undulating Carpet Path in summer.*

Bottom *Witty topiary details add structure and form to the Herb Garden.*

Top *Grey to Green streets are now beautiful corridors for wildlife, walkers, and cyclists.*

Bottom *Flower spires of eremurus catch the light in what is now a sociable space.*

GARDEN INSPIRATION

Natural Impact

This innovative scheme, now adopted by other local authorities, shows how high-impact, naturalistic displays of perennials can be used to fill awkward, utilitarian, or restricted spaces. Close planting reduces the need for weeding, rain provides the water, and low-maintenance herbaceous plants are cut back just once a year.

Grey to Green, Sheffield

WHERE *Inner-city Sheffield, particularly Castlegate S3* WHEN *Spring to autumn for displays of perennials and grasses* WHAT *A city-centre landscaping development creating new areas of public spaces and 0.8 miles (1.3km) of footpaths and cycleways*

This revolutionary plant-based scheme offers solutions to the practical challenges of climate change and urban decay. It has revitalized Sheffield city centre for people and wildlife, and brought beauty to the urban landscape through the power of plants.

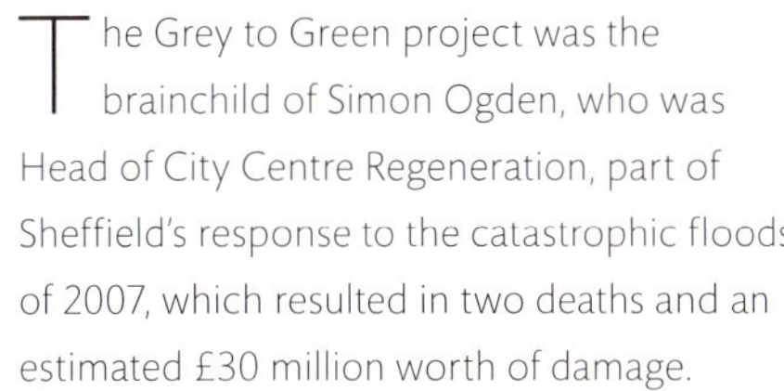

The Grey to Green project was the brainchild of Simon Ogden, who was Head of City Centre Regeneration, part of Sheffield's response to the catastrophic floods of 2007, which resulted in two deaths and an estimated £30 million worth of damage.

His innovative yet simple idea was to transform rundown streets into beautiful, flower-filled havens, so he approached Nigel Dunnett, Professor of Planting Design at the University of Sheffield, for help.

The process included a stretch of dual carriageway being turned into cycle and pedestrian paths and public spaces, then lined by sustainable borders to encourage public use. The impact has been transformational for people and the environment. Run-off water is absorbed by the borders and percolates back into the ground to prevent flash flooding, trees contribute to urban cooling, and the linear planting not only appeals to the public but has created a wildlife corridor. All this has encouraged businesses back to the area, inspiring urban regeneration.

POWERFUL PLANTS

The plants in these naturalistic schemes have been chosen for their tolerance of extreme conditions, wet and dry, and their ability to thrive in a specially engineered soil made of recycled compost and glass mixed with crushed sandstone and loam.

The textured planting is a mix of native and non-native species. Structural multi-stemmed trees and large shrubs are underplanted with a diverse range of seasonal perennials, from the spring-flowering pasqueflower and cowslip primroses, through spring and summer bulbs like lilies and alliums, to a wide range of robust, later-flowering daisies and ornamental grasses. *Carex testacea* provides year-round interest and contemporary street furniture complements the colour of the burnt-orange spires of *Eremurus* × *isabellinus* 'Cleopatra'.

Amid the planting, artistic, totem-like habitat shelters provide nesting space for pollinating insects as well as natural pest controllers – key to the 561 per cent increase in biodiversity here.

The Tea House nestles among the acers and ferns in Tatton Park's lush, tranquil Japanese Garden.

Tatton Park

WHERE *Knutsford, Cheshire, WA16 6SG* WHEN *Year-round interest; spring for flowering shrubs; summer for the Walled Garden; autumn for trees* WHAT *One of the finest examples of English parkland and garden landscapes, created over three centuries*

Tatton Park is a historical estate consisting of an 809-hectare (2,000-acre) deer park, a neoclassical mansion, and 20 hectares (49 acres) of ornamental, pleasure, and kitchen gardens. Once owned by the Egerton family for nearly 400 years, this magnificent estate blends classic English garden traditions with diverse cultural influences.

The magnificent park that extends outwards from the mansion owes much to the work of several eminent eighteenth-century landscape gardeners, including William Emes, John Webb, and Humphry Repton. In places, however, it has been overlaid by fine collections of Victorian-introduced North American conifers and Asian trees and shrubs, particularly rhododendrons, camellias, and magnolias.

The ornamental pleasure gardens positioned closer to the mansion came later and were designed, in part, by Joseph Paxton (see page 39), who laid out the Italian Garden in 1847 and was also responsible for the impressive Fernery, built in the 1850s to house a superb collection of Australasian tree ferns. Close by is the Grand Conservatory, which is stocked with oranges and lemons, clivias, passion flowers, and mimosa.

THE JAPANESE GARDEN

Today, Tatton is perhaps best known for its superb Japanese Garden, almost certainly designed following the 3rd Baron Egerton's visit to the Japan–British Exhibition at White City in London in 1910. The garden took three years to complete and is considered one of the finest Japanese gardens in Europe.

In the style of a tea garden, it features, among other things, a tea house, streams, pools, bridges, stone lanterns, carefully placed rocks, and even a stone representation of Mount Fuji. The garden was completely restored in the 1990s with the help of Japanese designers, and is undoubtedly one of the highlights of any visit.

KITCHEN STAPLES

In recent years, the 2-hectare (5-acre) Walled Garden has also taken centre stage. Having undergone extensive restoration, it takes you on a fascinating journey back in time to the heyday of British productive gardens, when estates like Tatton would have been completely self-sufficient in vegetables, fruit, and cut flowers.

The Orchard Garden grows over 85 apple and 40 pear varieties, while along the south-facing wall is a run of glasshouses, producing such delicacies as early and late grapes, peaches, nectarines, and apricots.

Top *Tom Stuart-Smith's Worsley Welcome Garden has a maze-like structure, softened with flowing herbaceous perennials.*

Bottom *The Walled Garden features* Coreopsis tripteris, Liatris pychnostachya, *and* Heuchera villosa *'Autumn Bride'.*

RHS Garden Bridgewater

WHERE *Worsley, Salford, Manchester, M28 2LJ* WHEN *All year round*
WHAT *Modern garden created by the Royal Horticultural Society in the footprint of a historic site*

Opened in 2021, this 62-hectare (154-acre) garden is one of Europe's largest garden projects, created within the historic footprint of Worsley New Hall. Development is ongoing, but highlights include the walled kitchen garden, Paradise Garden, and Chinese Streamside Garden.

Surely the most exciting garden project of recent years, RHS Garden Bridgewater is essentially a new garden that makes best use of the surviving features from the site's rich past, principally the former estate's 4.5-hectare (11-acre) walled kitchen gardens. The wider landscape includes woodland, meadows, two lakes, and former terraces that step up to where the now-demolished house once stood.

TV gardener Carol Klein remarked when opening the garden in 2021 that it "represents not only the spirit of the RHS, but that of the North West; pioneering and looking to the future". Certainly, the transformation from a somewhat overgrown site to a cutting-edge garden that embraces twenty-first-century values is remarkable.

A GARDEN FOR ALL

Visitors arrive through the elegantly modern Welcome Building, complete with green roof and rainwater harvesting positioned beside a new lake, Moon Bridge Water. Landscape architect Tom Stuart-Smith was appointed by the RHS in 2015 to draw up the garden's masterplan; he also developed the immersive Worsley Welcome Garden with massed *Sanguisorba*, *Rodgersia* and *Iris sibirica* planted in a maze of beds, like pieces of a mosaic.

Beside it, the Weston Walled Garden is subdivided into inner and outer areas, its restored brickwork furnished generously with climbers and trained fruit trees. Half the inner part contains the productive yet ornamental Kitchen Garden, including the forest garden,

TIMELINE OF EVENTS

1845

Worsley New Hall is completed.

1846

Landscape architect William Andrews Nesfield starts work on the gardens.

1857

The lake is enlarged.

1914–18

The house is used as a war hospital; decline of the gardens begins.

1943

Fire damages the house; demolition follows.

2015

RHS announces that the site is to become the fifth RHS Garden.

2016

RHS develops masterplan; planning permission is granted in 2017.

2017

Work begins on the Walled Garden.

2021

RHS Garden Bridgewater opens on 18 May.

2023

Blue Peter Discover Soil Garden opens and a music pavilion is erected in the Chinese Streamside Garden.

"This garden represents not only the spirit of the RHS, but that of the North West: pioneering and looking to the future."

CAROL KLEIN

Featuring a mix of Asiatic, North American, and Mediterranean plants and a tranquil pool, the Paradise Garden is a modern take on ancient designs.

herbal garden, and formal vegetable garden, while the serene Paradise Garden (also designed by Tom Stuart-Smith) fills the rest. Here, a lily pond is fed by rills that run along the garden's central axis, while geometric beds overflow with Mediterranean plants on one side, plants from Asia on the other, and from North America in the central area. Along the south-facing wall, lean-to glasshouses cascade with tender plants, including succulents, vines, and fruit trees. Outer areas include the Community Wellbeing Garden, with its contemplative spaces and raised beds for seasonal activities. Don't miss the Orchard Gardens beside the Gardener's Cottage, with local and heritage fruit trees and plantings for bees and butterflies, and the Old Frame Yard where RHS plant trials can be inspected.

Development outside the walled garden continues. The Chinese Streamside Garden and its meandering stream with pools, rocks, and a cascade, connects Ellesmere Lake to Moon Bridge Water. And there is more to come. Middle Wood is particularly interesting: the RHS aims to fuse the best a native British woodland can offer with additional exotic species to widen the season of interest and boost resilience. Further development includes the creation of four interlinked pavilions that will make up The Scholar's Garden.

FOCUS ON

Developing a Fifth RHS Garden

The RHS searched for a site to develop a fifth garden for over a decade; Bridgewater proved perfect, combining a mostly blank canvas with moist, mild conditions that suit many plants, not to mention the Walled Garden. The next phase of development is likely to include the creation of an arboretum, a new lakeside café, and possible renovation of the terraces.

Above *Joseph Paxton's bold nineteenth-century Rock Garden, now revitalized with modern perennial planting.*

Below *The magnificent Cascade, built in 1696, is Grade I listed and rises in 23 steps.*

Chatsworth

WHERE *Bakewell, Derbyshire, DE45 1PP* WHEN *Late spring until early autumn*
WHAT *Mainly "gardenesque" nineteenth-century garden with earlier features, within eighteenth-century parkland, with recent changes by contemporary designers: a fabulous jewel*

Walk the 42.5-hectare (105-acre) gardens at Chatsworth and experience 450 years of garden history, from the first Elizabethan layout, through the glory days of the 6th Duke of Devonshire and architect Joseph Paxton, to today's extensive naturalistic plantings.

Magnificent Chatsworth House is an undisputed national treasure. It is a place of great history and also constant evolution. Developments in recent years are keeping it relevant and inspirational, while ongoing restoration of its many outstanding features means visitors will enjoy its delights for generations to come.

ILLUSTRIOUS BEGINNINGS

Originally set out in Tudor times, the gardens we enjoy today really start with the 1st Duke of Devonshire (1641–1707). It was he who built the marvellous Cascade, the Willow Tree Fountain, and the elegant 1st Duke's Greenhouse, currently home to a fine camellia collection and flanked by a newly replanted rose garden.

A century later, in 1826, the 6th Duke (1811–1858) met a brilliant young gardener called Joseph Paxton. It was the start of a glorious relationship, Paxton over the years transforming the site and being largely responsible for some of Chatsworth's triumphs, including the monumental Rock Garden; the Emperor Fountain, which soars to 61 metres (200ft); and the now-lost Great Conservatory, once the largest glasshouse in the world.

A GARDEN FIT FOR THE FUTURE

Recent years have witnessed great changes. Paxton's remarkable Rock Garden has been remodelled and features wonderful perennial plantings, while new meadow-like glades have transformed the heart of the garden, known as Arcadia – including the 100 Steps Glade leading up from the Maze, with superb woodland-edge plantings by Tom Stuart-Smith, and Dan Pearson's redevelopment of the Trout Stream.

FOCUS ON

Joseph Paxton

Joseph Paxton was both a gardener and engineer, who was particularly interested in glasshouses. Advances in manufacturing allowed him to experiment at Chatsworth. As well as the Great Conservatory, he built a house for the first giant waterlily to flower in cultivation, using an innovative modular design with a ridge-and-furrow roof, seen later in his masterpiece, the Crystal Palace, for the 1851 Great Exhibition.

Acers shine with spectacular autumn colour in the China Garden, where the golden water buffalo sits in state.

FOCUS ON

James Bateman

James Bateman (1811–1897) was destined to garden. Aged eight, he fell in love with orchids and this passion would be lifelong. He published the ten-volume *Orchidaceae of Mexico and Guatemala* (1837–43), having begun a collection of tropical tree-dwelling (epiphytic) orchids. The 125 copies of his book contained life-size paintings as well as a wealth of scientific and cultural information.

Biddulph Grange

WHERE *Biddulph, Staffordshire, ST8 7SD* WHEN *All year round for structure; spring to autumn for seasonal interest and colour* WHAT *A Victorian masterpiece that draws inspiration from Italy, China, and Egypt for a playful, eccentric feel*

One of the most innovative gardens of the nineteenth century, Biddulph Grange was created by horticulturalist James Bateman in a High Victorian style, with theatrical tableaux and a wealth of new plant introductions celebrating the diversity of the botanical world.

Bateman was a devout Christian and a man of the Victorian scientific world, whose private income allowed him to concentrate on gardening and good works. In 1838 he married Maria Edgerton Warburton, a clergyman's daughter and keen gardener, whose relatives created the gardens at Arley Hall in Cheshire.

In the mid-nineteenth century, scientists were beginning to re-evaluate the natural world, and by creating a geological gallery and garden filled with botanical treasures introduced by the Victorian plant hunters, Bateman sought to reconcile the ideas of Creation and evolution. Over the next 27 years, helped by artist Edward Cooke, he created this idiosyncratic masterpiece.

GLOBAL INFLUENCES

A series of impressive subdivided terraces, including a colourful dahlia terrace and parterres, connect the Italianate mansion to the lake and parkland below. Other plantings include a Rhododendron Ground filled with early introductions from North America and the Caucasus; a Himalayan Glade – one of many examples of imposing rockwork; a "Wellingtonia Avenue", and the oldest stumpery in the country – all on a grand scale.

The Victorian obsession with Egypt and China is highlighted in two bold garden "rooms" with tableaux celebrating their cultures. In the China Garden, entry through a temple reveals a garden laid out like a Willow-pattern design, not in blue, but in vibrant oriental colours. Within there is a joss house, bridge, and pergola, and the most memorable feature: a gilded sacred water buffalo, perched on a wall under a canopy, overseeing the scene.

The Egypt-inspired garden is just as dramatic, where a central path divides a rectangular grass court flanked by topiary obelisks, with bases of golden yew and shafts of green yew. There are two pairs of stone sphinxes here, one guarding the entrance to the tunnel leading to a statue of the baboon Thoth, the Egyptian god of botany.

A melting pot of ideas, cultures, and plantsmanship, Biddulph Grange is a fascinating and majestic trip through the Victorian mind.

The scale and formality of the Italian Gardens is softened by contemporary plantings designed by Tom Stuart-Smith.

Trentham

WHERE *Trentham, Stoke-on-Trent, Staffordshire, ST4 8JG* WHEN *Year-round structure; February to May for extensive spring bulb interest and tree blossom; June to August for summer perennials, roses, and wisteria; September to October for autumn colour* WHAT *Formal gardens on a grand scale with parterres, contemporary borders, and lakeside landscaping*

This masterpiece of landscape design tells a compelling story of rise, decline, and spectacular rebirth. The historic estate of Trentham, spanning over 293 hectares (725 acres), represents one of the most remarkable garden restoration projects of the modern era.

Trentham's story as a significant landscape began in the eighteenth century when the 1st Duke of Sutherland commissioned Charles Bridgeman to design the formal gardens. However, it was "Capability" Brown (see page 60) in the 1760s who transformed Trentham into something extraordinary, with sweeping lawns, serpentine lake, and artfully placed trees. The work of both these notable landscape architects still forms the backbone of what we see today.

Trentham's true heyday, however, came in the Victorian era when the 2nd Duke hired Charles Barry, architect of London's Palace of Westminster, to create what became one of the most celebrated Victorian gardens in Britain. The Italian Gardens, which remain a centerpiece today, were designed to be viewed from the original mansion's windows, with elaborate parterres, fountains, and statuary creating a visual spectacular on a grand scale. Sadly, though, thanks to industrial pollution, the house was eventually abandoned and mostly knocked down in 1912. The second half of the twentieth century then saw the gardens fall into disrepair.

RESURRECTION

The turn of the millennium marked the start of Trentham's remarkable rebirth. Designer Tom Stuart-Smith (see page 68) reimagined the Italian Gardens, filling Charles Barry's formal beds with a naturalistic scheme of perennials and grasses. This bold fusion of Victorian structure and contemporary planting has become a model for heritage restoration.

The Eastern Pleasure Grounds were enhanced with the addition of the Floral Labyrinth, where winding paths meander through tall, colourful herbaceous beds, and the naturalistic Rivers of Grass, both designed by Piet Oudolf (see page 110). Woodland walks were reinstated, the mile-long lake's tranquility restored, allowing nature to reclaim the area. The Lakeside Walk was then developed with Nigel Dunnett (see page 30), incorporating ecological "modern meadow" planting. The ongoing partnership with Tom Stuart-Smith to refresh the Italian Garden with climate-resilient planting demonstrates that great gardens are never truly finished, they are always evolving.

Dorothy Clive Garden

WHERE *Willowbridge, Market Drayton, Staffordshire, TF9 4EU* WHEN *Year-round interest; spring for camellias; May and June for rhododendrons and azaleas; summer for roses*
WHAT *A transformed quarry garden full of familiar as well as unusual plants*

Originally created by Colonel Harry Clive as a restorative haven for his ailing wife, this tranquil space with views over three counties has an emotional pull, as well as displaying a stunning range of plants and focusing on public education.

Colonel Harry Clive took on a disused 1-hectare (2½-acre) gravel quarry in 1940, with the intention of transforming it into a glorious garden for his wife, Dorothy, who suffered from Parkinson's disease. Working with the sloping contours, Clive filled the quarry with interconnecting paths and woodland plants, particularly acers and rhododendrons, to provide beautiful walks for Dorothy. The garden continued to expand after her death in 1942, and now covers almost 5 hectares (13 acres).

A GARDENER'S GARDEN

An impressive array of mature rhododendrons and azaleas illuminate the garden in spring – some of them chosen by Clive's friend Frank Knight, former director of RHS Garden Wisley, who was an authority on both plant groups. Noteworthy species include *Rhododendron thomsonii*, renowned for its blood-red flowers and peeling bark, and *Rhododendron orbiculare*, a compact plant with rose-pink, bell-like blooms. A collection of azaleas sent from Lord Rothschild during the Second World War from his own gardens at Exbury near Southampton included two excellent hybrids that would be named after their new custodians, the pale-pink 'Dorothy Clive' and vibrant orange 'The Colonel'.

Many different plant groups are represented in the various areas of the garden, among them the Alpine Scree, Rock Garden, Herbaceous Borders, Sun Terrace, and Dry Garden. There are fine displays of roses, including RHS Award of Garden Merit (AGM) winners, as well as a Camellia and Azalea Walk, Winter Garden, and Edible Woodland, planted with layers of shade-tolerant plants, from tuberous vegetables, to herbs, to shrub fruits, to cropping trees.

Alongside the mature oaks, which provide shade for understorey plantings in the Quarry Garden, there are many specimen trees, some of them unusual and highly desirable, such as *Gymnocladus dioica* (the Kentucky coffee tree), *Trochodendron aralioides* (a horticultural curiosity from Japan and Korea), and the deciduous conifer *Metasequoia glyptostroboides*.

Now run by the Willoughbridge Garden Trust, the garden pursues the Colonel's wishes that it should be for public education as well as enjoyment. With its programme of workshops and exhibitions, particularly for young people, it's an all-seasons garden for the mind and soul.

Clockwise from top left
Flowers of Rhododendron orbiculare, *one of the garden's notable species.*

Mature azaleas and rhododendrons bring glorious colour to woodland walks.

Purple allium flowers complement the laburnum arch in full bloom.

FOCUS ON

Sustainability

The ethos at the Dorothy Clive Garden is to be sustainable and environmentally aware. As such, the Royal Botanic Glasshouse, with its bougainvillea, lemon trees, and living wall, is unheated and the structure second-hand, while the Laburnum Arch, underplanted with alliums, is constructed from a preloved polytunnel.

Clockwise from top left

Cascading wisteria blooms signal the way to the Secret Garden.

The drifts of Tulipa sprengeri *have been decades in the making.*

Neatly regimented veg beds are a nod back to the monastic farm.

GARDEN INSPIRATION

The Gift of Time

Stockton Bury is well known for its drifts of the rare *Tulipa sprengeri*. The first bulbs were given to the owners 50 years ago by Christopher Lloyd. These tiny species tulips take decades to bulk up, the secret being to avoid deadheading. They now run through the borders like a red ribbon in late May. This is planting that can't be rushed – time is the secret to success.

Stockton Bury Gardens

WHERE *Kimbolton, Leominster, Hereford, HR6 0HB* WHEN *From April to the end of September*
WHAT *A plant collector's garden created at the heart of a working farm*

Over 25 years ago this 1.6-hectare (4-acre) garden was opened to the public. It remains a private home and the passion of its owners and creators, Raymond Treasure and Gordon Fenn.

Herefordshire is a county associated with farming, and this garden doesn't waver from that; it's been created on the site of what was once a monastic farm. On arrival, visitors are greeted by a view of the cider orchards where sheep happily graze below the branches of these productive trees. Wall shrubs and generously planted borders cushion the medieval pigeon house, stables, tithe barn, and cider press. Although rich in history, most of the garden is only 50 years old.

Embracing tradition with sensitivity, however, is key in this garden. Owner Raymond Treasure is the fourth generation of his family to reside here. His ancestors planted what is now the largest monkey puzzle tree in Herefordshire, in 1894. Today, the garden is renowned for being home to many rare and unusual plants. At every turn there are specimens that outwit even the most passionate plantspeople.

NATURAL DEVELOPMENT

Inspired by his second cousin, John Treasure (well known for his expertise in clematis), and John's great friend Christopher Lloyd (see page 84), Raymond's hobby quickly got out of hand and the garden at Stockton Bury expanded into the surrounding fields and paddocks.

There was no masterplan; instead, the garden developed organically over time. The site is made up of several garden "rooms", all offering visitors take-home ideas. Key to its success is that priority is given to the "right plant, right place" principle. It is a masterclass in what to grow where and demonstrates that by planting in the right place you can even have kiwis, peaches, cherries, and apricots in a Herefordshire garden.

Wisteria decorates the house and stables and is a feature of the well-hidden Secret Garden, which offers views of the Black Mountains. The Spring Garden is a picture when *Fritillaria meleagris* creates drifts below the traditional bee bole wall. The Iris Walk and Pillar Gardens feature a relay of herbaceous perennials throughout summer, and at the very far end of the garden, in the Dingle, a stream tumbles into a large pond. In April the banks are lit up by drifts of *Anemone nemorosa* and in May candelabra primulas dance along the edge of the stream, while mature *Cornus kousa* offers shelter to the many shade-loving plants.

Red-brick tower follies offer glorious views over the garden, where hedging adds a sense of seclusion at ground level.

Stone House Cottage Garden & Nursery

WHERE *Church Lane, Kidderminster, Worcestershire, DY10 4BG* WHEN *From spring to late summer* WHAT *A private garden, created on the site of an old kitchen garden, which is a showcase for the adjoining specialist nursery*

Within the walls of Louisa Arbuthnott's private garden, there's a collection of plants that even the most seasoned fanatic might struggle to identify. This is the place to see rare and unusual wall shrubs, climbers, and herbaceous perennials growing in their full glory.

Stone House Cottage is a hidden gem and a plant hunter's paradise. It might only be 0.4 hectares (1 acre), but once inside, it seems much bigger. Originally a walled garden, though one that is open on the west side, allowing for good air circulation, it was transformed by owners Louisa Arbuthnott and her late husband, James, in 1975.

The couple bought the house purely for the garden, which was then dedicated to productive vegetable growing. For them, it was a passion project and wasn't heavily designed - its main purpose was as a family garden, but also as a showcase for plants, where they could test the boundaries of what could grow in Worcestershire.

Notable features in the garden are the follies that James built against the original walls. He discovered a love for bricklaying, and so it was he who planned the architectural space while Louisa was to plant it. The garden is often referred to as "the San Gimignano of the Midlands" thanks to the distinctive Italianate red-brick structures, some of which have arches and others windows. You enter the garden through one of these follies, which heightens the sense of exploration. In May, this entrance is dramatically covered in wisteria.

A PLANT LOVER'S PARADISE

Dividing up the garden with hedges to create vistas has served Stone House Cottage well and given Louisa maximum scope for planting. The result is a romantic country garden that's a jewel box of plants. It's impossible to stroll past a border without stopping to closely admire a mystery specimen. Thankfully they are all labelled, and Louisa is on hand to give advice.

Her love of plants began when she was a teenager, and she admits that her plant interests are continually changing. One plant group that

Clockwise from top *Monarda and nepeta scent the way to a brick folly.*

Pastel tones cool down this double border in high summer.

The meadow area with mown paths.

"I am interested in garden-worthy plants that bring something special to a garden, rather than being a botanical collector."

LOUISA ARBUTHNOTT

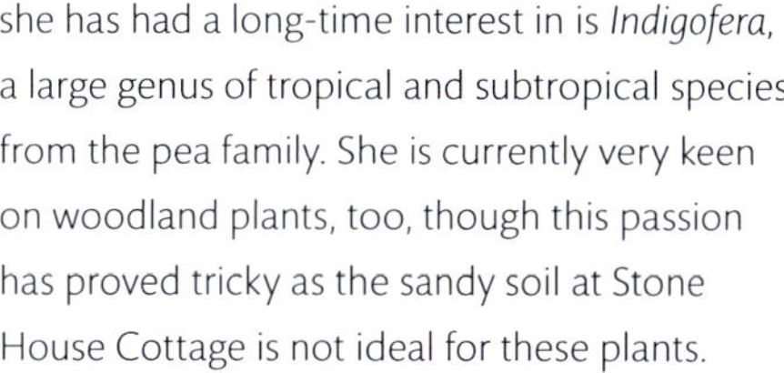

she has had a long-time interest in is *Indigofera*, a large genus of tropical and subtropical species from the pea family. She is currently very keen on woodland plants, too, though this passion has proved tricky as the sandy soil at Stone House Cottage is not ideal for these plants.

When creating the garden Louisa was quick to decorate the follies and walls with a collection of unusual climbers, since the garden was to act as a shop window for her adjoining nursery, where all the plants are propagated by her. It's Louisa's encyclopaedic knowledge of plants that has earned this garden its stellar reputation. Gardener and author Roy Lancaster once wrote in *The Garden* that "Louisa seems to have a remarkable way with plants, especially the more desirable ones, and is not intimidated by a plant's recalcitrant reputation." Louise is quick to admit, however, that she isn't a botanist: "I am interested in garden-worthy plants that bring something special to a garden, rather than being a botanical collector."

INSPIRING IDEAS

There are many different routes around the garden, with some taking you under yew arches, which are often placed at the end of a double border like a full stop, while others lead to the meadow planting. This naturalistic area, on the left as you enter the garden, with grass paths running through it, features the all-important yellow rattle, which allows orchids and ox-eye daisies to compete with the meadow grasses.

At every turn are plantings that will leave visitors enthused to try them at home – the yellow and white border, for example, featuring contrasting flower shapes as well as colours. Phlox mingle with the spikes of white flowers from the veronicastrum and the tiny, bright-white blooms of thalictrum. Elsewhere in the shade beds, foliage is king. With every inch planted up with glorious colour, form, and texture, it's no surprise that there's never a lull in the garden from spring through to late summer.

FOCUS ON

Walled Gardens

To have a garden protected by walls not only reduces the chance of rabbits entering, but also allows more tender climbers to grow. A south-facing wall acts as a radiator, protecting less hardy specimens. Tender perennials will also thrive at the foot of a wall under the rain shadow.

Hill Close Gardens

WHERE *Warwick, CV34 6HF* WHEN *Spring, summer, and autumn* WHAT *A series of historically important Victorian "detached gardens", saved from redevelopment in the 1990s*

"Detached gardens" were commonplace in the Victorian era, but sadly today most have been swept away. Hill Close Gardens is a rare survivor just a short walk from Warwick town centre, and makes a fascinating place to visit for its rich social history.

Many gardens open to the public are famed for their plant collections, grandiose features, or impressive design. Hill Close Gardens offers a refreshing contrast. It consists of individual plots, which were leased, or later bought freehold, often by families of tradesmen, who lived in premises above local shops or businesses without gardens. They were similar to allotments, but used as "detached gardens" for recreation and relaxation, as well as growing produce. Many also featured marvellous brick summerhouses.

Although such plots were once common, Hill Close is one of just five similar sites now remaining; its survival shows us something of how ordinary people once gardened, shedding light on a past now all but forgotten.

HUMAN STORIES

The gardens are positioned on a slope, today overlooking Warwick Racecourse. Originally there were 32 plots, and while many have been lost, 16 remain, with details known about the families who gardened there. They are separated by hedges and reached by narrow alleyways that cross the site; each retains its historic plot number and has its own layout. Plot 17, for example, is one of the largest, with a grand summerhouse and stone paths. For 40 years it belonged to James Styles, a shoemaker and later owner of a large furniture store.

Plot 19 includes a charming hexagonal summerhouse, now lovingly restored, which belonged until 1898 to a publican. It was later owned by a greengrocer and used as a market garden – as a result it includes many fruit trees. Plot 24 is the only one to have been gardened continuously – in 1870, it featured four plum trees, three standard and one espalier apple, and numerous soft fruit bushes.

Across the gardens today grow many heritage vegetables and 70 cultivars of apple. You'll find a border of Victorian plants and others housing a Plant Heritage National Collection of Chrysanthemums, which provides dazzling colour in autumn. Spring is welcomed by snowdrops, of which 140 selections can be found. Yet it's the human stories that resonate most; today we know that gardening has many health benefits, but it's clear those who used these plots as an escape from the stresses of everyday life decades ago realized it, too.

Clockwise from right

In autumn, summer flowers still abound alongside ripening fruit.

Enchanting Victorian summerhouses still survive in several garden plots.

The gardens were restored first by volunteers, then National Lottery funding.

FOCUS ON

Sophisticated Summerhouses

Detached gardens often included brick-built summerhouses. They offered shelter in bad weather and, as most featured a small fire to heat up a meal, provide a hot drink, or dry gardening clothes, they could be kept warm well into the evening, allowing people to work in their gardens all day. Four of the summerhouses at Hill Close are Grade II listed; two even have cellars used to store fruit.

Thenford Arboretum & Gardens

WHERE *Thenford, Banbury, OX17 2BX* WHEN *February for snowdrops; April to May for blossom; July to August for herbaceous beds; October for autumn colour*
WHAT *A private arboretum and garden with beautifully restored historic features, impressive collections, and quirky details*

Extending to over 28 hectares (70 acres), Thenford has been lovingly developed by Michael and Anne Heseltine over the last 50 years. Its notable collection of unusual trees, wonderful plantings, and sculpture collection have rightly earned it great acclaim.

There can be no doubt that the gardens at Thenford have become an all-consuming passion for the Heseltines. When they arrived in 1976, they found the woodland overgrown, the lake and medieval fish ponds silted up, and the Walled Garden given over to pasture. Over five decades, however, they transformed the historic bones of the grounds, as well as adding new garden spaces to complement the existing woodland and enhance the Walled Garden.

HISTORIC TRANSFORMATIONS

To the south of the eighteenth-century house, a wide expanse of lawn slopes down to the fully restored lake, which reflects light into the open woodlands that appear to wrap in close to each end of the building. Here, planting is simple, with shade-loving shrubs, bulbs, and herbaceous plants creating the understorey to a mix of mature trees and younger plantings.

A path to the east of the house cuts through the trees, the gentle slope running uphill through a series of garden rooms that appear like woodland glades. These house the eclectic mix of sculptures, by artists including Elisabeth Frink, Lynn Chadwick, and Michael Ayrton.

Water forms the life force of the garden. The path then crosses a stream, which transforms into a series of water features, starting with the spectacular formal cascade known as the Rill. A series of large ponds then feed the elegant Water Gardens, before the stream flows through the Chinese Garden, to the Bog Garden.

There is more to come in the Walled Garden, productive once more. The diamond chequerboard of beds, lawns, and clipped hedging is dotted with pavilions, fruit cages, and aviaries, while the grand double borders of the Herbaceous Walk on the south side of the walled area are bursting with colour in the summer months.

All of this forms part of the extensive Arboretum of more than 3,500 unusual woody plants, including over 100 champion trees (see page 93), which will become the lasting legacy of this husband-and-wife partnership.

Crossing one of the medieval fish ponds, the Blue Bridge creates an eye-catching accent of colour, even in the depths of winter.

Modelled on arid Arizona, the flint-lined channels of the Desert Wash draw rainfall from the drought-tolerant plantings.

East Ruston Old Vicarage Garden

WHERE *East Ruston, Norfolk, NR12 9HN* WHEN *Year-round interest; March to May for spring bulbs and blossom; July to September for flowers and innovative container displays* WHAT *An eclectic mix of garden rooms, arranged mostly in strong geometric forms radiating from the house*

Created from scratch by Alan Gray and Graham Robeson since 1973, this garden has become one of the UK's most visited. Its success demonstrates how dedication, expertise, and a clear vision can transform even an unprepossessing plot into a garden of dreams.

The extraordinary genesis of the exotic, complex garden at East Ruston Old Vicarage, created in open fields close to the North Norfolk coast, is a testament to its colourful owners. Initially, only the 0.8 hectares (2 acres) that came with the house were gardened, but more land was purchased from 1989, and a decision made to replant old hedge boundaries. With this division of the plot came a plan to develop distinct garden rooms, and to recreate the wildlife habitats that had been swept away by intensive farming.

WORLD CLASS

The garden now extends to 13 hectares (32 acres) and incorporates a diverse collection of spaces that take visitors all over the world. The grand Diamond Jubilee Walled Garden feels quintessentially English, with its central pergola draped in climbing roses, flanked by cutting flowers, fruit cages, and herb beds. The Desert Wash, meanwhile, mimics an Arizona landscape, with drought-tolerant plants hailing from California, Africa, and South America, and the south-facing terraces of the Mediterranean Garden feature heat-loving plants such as *Echium pininana* from the Canary Islands. Other gardens are formed with hedges, such as the Sunk Garden, where raised beds of exuberant plantings sit alongside alpine troughs and water features; the Dutch Garden, where a box parterre sets off stunning tulip displays; and the Exotic Garden, where cannas, *Musa basjoo*, bamboo, and palms bring colour and structure in defiance of the harsh coastal climate.

Many more areas are divided and crossed by long paths to create vistas, such as the King's Walk, Clematis Walk, and Apple Walk. The latter has a borrowed view to Happisburgh village church, while the Winter Garden affords a glimpse of a splendid lighthouse by the sea-cliff edge. Such scenes only add to this masterpiece of a garden, which is constantly being refined within its well-defined bones.

Dogwood bushes create a seam of gold through the grasses and seedheads of the Winter Garden.

The Bressingham Gardens

WHERE *Diss, Norfolk, IP22 2AA* WHEN *From mid-February to the end of March to see winter planting at its best; late summer for ornamental grasses; autumn for foliage colour* WHAT *A series of interlinked gardens, offering a rich plant portfolio in every season*

Over three generations, the Bloom family have created not just one garden but six at Bressingham. The initial aim was to show off their nursery stock, but over the years their experimentation has led to the garden and family being held in high horticultural esteem.

The Bressingham story began in 1953 when the founder of the family nursery, the late Alan Bloom – prolific plant breeder, writer, and steam-train enthusiast – created the Dell Garden in front of Bressingham Hall to showcase the nursery's wide selection of plants. He pioneered a new planting style by putting his ever-growing collection in island beds, and the concept quickly became celebrated.

Today, on what was once meadowland, there are six linked gardens over 6.8 hectares (17 acres), forming a unique destination that deserves a visit in every season.

BREAKING NEW GROUND

Growing plants in a different way didn't stop with the Dell Garden. When Alan's son Adrian Bloom joined the family nursery business in 1962 he started to create his own garden, Foggy Bottom, in which he experimented with year-round colour, primarily using conifers and heathers. His ground-breaking plantings gained the attention of the gardening media, and today the conifers and heathers are mixed with ornamental grasses and perennials. It is here that the vast diversity in shape, colour, and form within conifers is celebrated.

The Summer Garden joined the portfolio in 2001 and is home to the National Collection of *Miscanthus*. The planting is a powerful mix of perennials and grasses, a notable feature being the "river" of *Geranium* 'Rozanne'. The beds are generously planted with distinctive drifts surrounded by grass paths.

Another summer treasure is the Fragrant Garden, packed with perfumed delights. This links Foggy Bottom to Adrian's Wood, which is home to a collection of North American plants. In late summer and early autumn it offers a much-photographed scene of golden foliage. The seasonal interest is far from over, however, as the Winter Garden is a masterclass. Grasses mingle with colourful conifers, the red stems of cornus, and the silver trunks of *Betula*. This influential horticultural family continues to add new chapters to its story.

A double view of the eighteenth-century domed Archer Pavilion reflected in the Long Water.

FOCUS ON

Capability Brown

Renowned landscape architect Lancelot "Capability" Brown's (1716–1783) style was to create a refined form of the English landscape, with its smooth, rolling hills, carefully placed woodlands, and "natural" rivers and lakes, to create pastoral scenes that epitomized "nature perfected". He spoke of the "capabilities" or potential he saw in the existing landscape, hence his nickname.

Wrest Park

WHERE *Silsoe, Luton, Bedfordshire, MK45 4HR* WHEN *All year round; summer for floral displays, especially in the Italian Garden* WHAT *A formal landscape covering 37 hectares (92 acres), with outstanding structures, and ornamental features including a Rococo parterre and Walled Garden.*

The gardens at Wrest Park are one of the most complete remaining early-eighteenth-century formal landscapes, marking every major development in English garden design until the mid-nineteenth century. There is also an abundance of horticultural interest.

Wrest Park was owned by the de Grey family for nearly 700 years, and during that time, there were three key stages in its history: the creation of a formal woodland by Henry, Duke of Kent, from 1706; changes made under Jemima, Marchioness Grey, in the latter half of the 1700s; and the work of her grandson, Thomas, Earl de Grey, from 1833.

The family commissioned some of the most famous names in English gardening to develop Wrest Park: Batty Langley, Thomas Archer, and Thomas Wright. When the Marchioness employed Capability Brown (see opposite) to soften the edges of the park in 1758, few changes were made other than the construction of a serpentine lake, ensuring that earlier developments were preserved, not swept away.

SEASONAL DELIGHTS

Although Wrest Park is primarily a landscape garden, with its statuary, Long Water, and the magnificent baroque Archer Pavilion, there is plenty to draw in plant lovers.

Spring in the Woodland is heralded by snowdrops, daffodils, and primroses, accompanied by the spidery flowers and spicy scent of witch hazel. The delightfully fragranced wintersweet grows against a sheltered wall in the Pear Orchard, and a chocolate-scented *Azara microphylla* in the Rose Garden border. The 1836 Walled Garden is filled with fruit blossom, and the emerging foliage of perennial vegetables. Against the outside is an espaliered Judas tree, believed to be over 150 years old.

The conservatory is full of camellias in bloom, while the restored Italian Garden and parterres around the house are a riot of seasonal tulips, hyacinths, violas, forget-me-nots, and crown imperial fritillaries.

In summer, the displays in the Italian Garden shift to vibrantly coloured verbenas, cannas, pelargoniums, nicotianas, marigolds, ageratums, and salvias. The subtropical planting in the conservatory is at its best at this time of year, too, with lush banana plants, ginger lilies, and cannas. Outdoors, the Rose Garden is filled with a range of hybrid shrub roses for colour and fragrance from early summer until late autumn.

As the year draws to a close, there is a vivid display of autumn colour in the woodlands, while in winter the specimen trees and avenue of limes display their delicate tracery.

Clockwise from top *The Water Garden, ideal for aquatic plants and moisture-loving perennials.*

In the Gravel Garden, grasses and perennial alstroemeria flourish without extra irrigation.

Spring-flowering Leucojum aestivum *(snowflake) thrives in moist locations.*

Beth Chatto Gardens

WHERE *Elmstead Market, Colchester, Essex, CO7 7DB* WHEN *Spring, summer, and autumn* WHAT *Informal, innovative garden with five distinct areas, each demonstrating the principle of "right plant, right place"*

Beth Chatto was a pioneering gardener and nurserywoman who planted to suit the conditions she encountered. Her beautiful and inspiring garden, in the driest part of the UK, includes a woodland garden, water gardens, and the famous Gravel Garden, which is never irrigated.

Despite gardening on parched, sandy soil, Beth Chatto managed to create a beautiful, relaxed garden of world renown by carefully selecting plants she knew could adapt to her conditions. She also made use of the features to hand, such as a natural spring, which feeds several pools in her Water Garden.

To the east of the house, beside the excellent plant nursery, lies the sunny Scree Garden, its low, circular beds filled with drought-tolerant treasures – alpines or small plants easily lost in garden borders. To the west lies the lush Water Garden with pools and broad, grassed paths. Around pond margins are plants adapted to wet conditions, while aquatic irises and exotic *Thalia* emerge from the shallows.

INSPIRATION FOR SUN OR SHADE

The Reservoir Garden is an open, sunny space with island beds where drifts of grasses mingle with perennials in prairie-style plantings. It's impressive in summer and autumn, although in late spring look out for a fine multi-stemmed *Cercis* (Judas tree) wreathed with pink flowers. Spring is also perfect for the Woodland Garden, a masterclass in how to deal with dry shade. Here, bulbs are followed by perennials such as trilliums and epimediums carpeting the woodland floor. Later in the year, follow the winding paths for lush ferns, Japanese anemones, dazzling colchicums, and fiery autumn foliage.

RIGHT PLANT, RIGHT PLACE

The ultimate expression of Beth's "right plant, right place" principle is the superb Gravel Garden. The ethos is that while the sandy soil is improved with organic matter and mulched with gravel to retain moisture, the area is not watered after planting. It sounds dubious to the uninitiated, but the effects are so revelatory you'll wonder why you ever worried about hosepipe bans. The dazzling planting revels in the summer heat, *Agapanthus*, *Cistus*, and *Yucca* arranged in meandering borders that suggest a dry river bed, and it shines all year – even in winter, when seedheads sparkle with frost.

Drought-tolerant plants thrive among the boulders of the Dry Garden.

RHS Garden Hyde Hall

WHERE *Chelmsford, Essex, CM3 8ET* WHEN *All year round* WHAT *Expansive rural garden of varying styles, including semi-formal hilltop gardens and more naturalistic areas*

In recent years RHS Garden Hyde Hall has gone from strength to strength, using its challenging site conditions and rural setting to best advantage. While established areas include many traditional features, others bring inspiration and innovation.

This marvellous garden deserves greater recognition, for it is one of the most rewarding and relaxing sites to visit, with a collection of areas featuring varied planting styles and offering fine panoramas across the Essex landscape. The original garden has grown considerably since the RHS took on the site; today you'll find an inspiring Winter Garden, establishing woodland and a reservoir, the flower-filled Sky Meadow, and, as you climb up to the traditionally styled Hilltop Garden, sweeping Clover Hill borders with their naturalistic plantings, which fit perfectly into the landscape.

Developed from a working farm from the mid-1950s by gardeners Dick and Helen Robinson, the original garden was made on the higher ground around the old farmhouse with ponds and herbaceous borders dug, sheltering trees planted, and rose gardens started. The garden is in one of the driest parts of the UK with heavy clay soil, which brings both challenges and opportunities. In the early 1990s, the site was donated to the RHS. Today it has grown to 148 hectares (365 acres) of garden and surrounding grass and farmland.

GROWTH AND EVOLUTION

Beside the garden's entrance lie the Courtyard Gardens, comprising a Modern Country Garden with clipped geometric forms that contrast with a blend of perennials and grasses, and the Cottage Garden with its carefree planting. The Winter Garden is one of Hyde Hall's outstanding areas, with a path winding between expansive borders of winter-interest plants grown for stem colour, scent, flowers, or foliage. A particular feature is the extraordinary living sculptures created annually from coppiced willows.

The Dry Garden takes its cue from the nearby Beth Chatto Gardens (see page 62), but Hyde Hall's version provides a contrasting rendition, constructed on the sunny side of the hilltop with views to the lake and rural

Clockwise from top left
Living willow sculptures are created every autumn and winter for display.

The glasshouse and veg beds in the Global Growth Vegetable Garden.

The sunny Clover Hill borders feature informal drifts of grasses and herbaceous perennials.

landscape beyond. Paths step down between boulders that help retain soil, while plants from the Mediterranean and other arid areas abound, thriving from the garden's low rainfall and open conditions. It's an exciting place, the planting very much at home, with billowing nepeta and grasses such as *Stipa tenuissima* alongside *Verbascum*, *Euphorbia*, and *Yucca*. In spring, bulbous alliums and *Scilla peruviana* shine, while summer introduces dazzling orange Californian poppies and inky agapanthus. You'll also spot the unexpected, such as prickly pear cacti and succulent *Agave*.

There is masses to enjoy at Hyde Hall. Don't miss the circular Global Growth Vegetable Garden, added in 2017, featuring a host of unusual edible crops, some grown within a central glasshouse; the Robinson Garden with its gabion walls and bog plantings; the sloping Australia and New Zealand Garden, designed around several established *Eucalyptus* trees and packed with plants native to Australasia; the Queen Mother's Garden with its exotic planting, and the Rose Rope Walk with climate-resilient climbing roses trained on a metal framework.

GARDEN INSPIRATION

Winter Interest

Hyde Hall's Winter Garden shines for months. In autumn, *Pennisetum* and *Deschampsia* teem with seedheads, and the ornamental crab apples add glistening colour. In winter, scented *Chimonanthus*, *Daphne*, *Sarcococca*, and *Viburnum* can be enjoyed alongside dazzling stems of *Salix*, *Rubus*, and *Cornus*, which, in spring, are complemented by snowdrops, crocuses, and scilla.

TIMELINE OF EVENTS

1955

Helen and Dick Robinson arrive at Hyde Hall, then a working farm.

1963

Shelter belts are planted and the Woodland Garden started.

1976

Hyde Hall Gardens Trust is established.

1979

The Hilltop Garden with ponds is defined.

1993

The estate is donated to the RHS.

2001

The Dry Garden is completed.

2002

The Queen Mother's Garden is made.

2012

The Courtyard Gardens are made.

2017

The Global Growth Vegetable Garden is added.

2018

The Winter Garden is created.

FOCUS ON

Broughton's New Parterre

The design of historic parterre gardens was often inspired by patterns found in the home, such as embroidery or carvings. Tom Stuart-Smith based the pattern traced in wavy clipped dwarf euonymus in the Walled Garden parterre on the microscopic leaf structure of native beech, ash, and oak trees. The compartments are planted with 12 varieties of 5,000 tulips for joyous spring colour, followed by single plantings of bedding plants based on key genera, including *Brassica*, *Diascia*, and *Heliotropium*.

Top *The Upper Terrace has a prairie feel, with grasses, salvias, and asters.*

Bottom *Beech topiary is softened by perennials in the Middle Terrace.*

Broughton Grange

WHERE *Banbury, Oxfordshire, OX15 5DS* WHEN *Spring for tulips; summer for wildflowers and tapestry planting; all seasons for topiary and trees* WHAT *An ambitious mix of traditional and contemporary elements, including an inspiring Walled Garden on three levels, with views across an Oxfordshire valley*

Stunningly transformed since 1992 by its present owner Stephen Hester, Broughton Grange's extensive gardens continue to be developed and expanded, incorporating both formal and informal design elements.

The rolling farmland surrounding Broughton Grange is an all-important feature of this 10-hectare (25-acre) garden in rural Oxfordshire. *Allées*, breaks in hedges, and pairs of sentinel trees all frame views out to the meadows, fields, and hilltop trees that create its glorious setting.

The diversity of the garden's areas reflects the owner's delight in horticultural variety. Aspects of its Victorian origins have been retained and enhanced: an arboretum, started in 2003, creates a continuation of the mature parkland trees. The Victorian concept of using peat bricks to create the ideal conditions for ericaceous plants has been introduced in the Peat Terrace, where rhododendrons, daphnes, dogwoods, and Japanese maples thrive.

The layout of the 2019 Fountain Garden mirrors Baroque garden-making, while the design of the parterre in the adjoining Rose Garden, where 16 beds edged in *Euonymus japonicus* 'Jean Hughes' make up its linear pattern, was inspired by a visit to the Château de Villandry in France. English country garden elements, such as herbaceous long borders, a laburnum tunnel, and a wisteria-draped pergola, contrast with the informality of wildflower meadows and a wetland wilderness.

WALLED GARDEN REIMAGINED

The garden's most dramatic transformation is undoubtedly the sloping field to the east of the house that has been reimagined by designer Tom Stuart-Smith as a walled garden on three levels, where topiary yew and hornbeam echo and frame the verticals in the distant landscape.

On the Upper Terrace, Mediterranean planting fills a deep border alongside one wall, while vegetables and herbs encircle a striking circular fruit cage. A rill, bordered by prairie-style planting, drops down to the Middle Terrace, where stepping stones allow the visitor to float across the formal pool. The view south is across the colourful tapestry of the Parterre (see opposite) on the Lower Terrace and, below it, the rounded forms of topiary yew that cast long shadows across the close-cut lawn.

The Palladian Bridge straddles an arm of the Octagon Lake and leads up to the Gothic Temple.

Stowe Gardens

WHERE *Buckingham, Buckinghamshire, MK18 5EQ* WHEN *All year round for vistas, garden buildings, and monuments* WHAT *A masterpiece in creative landscaping on a majestic scale, ideal for long walks and autumn colour*

At the great estate of Stowe, what appears to be natural is entirely made by hand. This is landscape gardening on a majestic scale, incorporating the work of some of Britain's most famous landscape designers and architects.

Stowe's 304 hectares (750 acres) of parkland are the setting for one of the grandest of grand designs, with both house and grounds conceived on a vast scale.

What began as a traditional formal landscape was transformed under Stowe's fifth owner, 1st Viscount Cobham, in the early eighteenth century. During his time, the landscape was moulded in a naturalistic style, aimed at demonstrating the perfection of nature, by a team of over 30 gardeners. Cobham oversaw the creation of the garden as both a responder to taste and a taste-maker, employing a succession of artists and craftsmen who would become famous for their designs. John Vanbrugh, Charles Bridgeman, William Kent, and "Capability" Brown (see page 60) all played vital roles in Stowe's development.

Such a project was quite a feat. The Grecian Valley, the last section to be completed under the direction of Capability Brown (who in the 1740s was head gardener and clerk of all works) and Cobham, with its naturalized lakes and temples, was formed by 500 men using hand tools.

A MONUMENTAL LANDSCAPE

The gardens at Stowe are renowned for their monuments and buildings - over 50 in all - many of them designed with hidden symbolism or thinly veiled political comment. The Temple of Ancient Virtue, for example, is an homage to Socrates, Homer, Lycurgus, and Epaminondas, whom Cobham believed embodied virtues lacking in public figures of his day. Other buildings of note include the Chinese House, attributed to William Kent and the earliest surviving Chinese-style pavilion in Britain.

What is too often overlooked, however, is the number of significant trees at Stowe. The Tree Register records around 200 notable specimens. There are 24 Buckinghamshire County champions, including the large cedar near the Temple of Concord and Victory, and the largest tree in a rare avenue of 60 *Fagus sylvatica* 'Dawyck' north-west of the gothic church. The *Ginkgo biloba* just below the athletics track on the edge of the Grecian Valley, with a trunk nearly 4 metres (13ft) in circumference, is well worth seeking out.

Waterperry Gardens

WHERE *Waterperry, Wheatley, Oxfordshire, OX33 1JZ* WHEN *Year-round interest; spring for the fritillary meadow and spring to autumn for the herbaceous border* WHAT *A garden with an influential history, fine displays of fruit and vegetables, and a magnificent herbaceous border*

Beatrix Havergal and her partner Avice Sanders started a School of Horticulture for Ladies at Pusey House near Faringdon in 1927, but it became so successful that by 1932 they had moved to larger premises at Waterperry House, near Oxford, where they could expand their vision.

After five years of clearing trees for ornamentals and improving the soil for crop production, Havergal and Sanders had transformed Waterperry into a thriving school and garden. The syllabus covered all aspects of theory and practice, from ornamentals to fruit, vegetables, and greenhouse production, and students became highly skilled "all-rounders". This diversity is still seen at Waterperry.

USEFUL AND BEAUTIFUL

Havergal was famous for her gold-medal-winning 'Royal Sovereign' strawberries at the Chelsea Flower Show, and fruit remains a feature here. There are 2 hectares (5 acres) of productive orchards growing some 60 apple varieties, seasonal plums, greengages, and rare pears. There are also well-grown vegetables and dahlias in the Walled Garden.

There are virtuosic displays of ornamentals here, too. Alpines – a specialism of horticulturist and photographer Valerie Finnis, who was a notable alumna of the school – are displayed in the Alpine and Rock Garden. There is also a National Collection of two groups of saxifrage, a fritillary meadow, which is at its peak in spring, and a young arboretum, planted with an eye to the future. The island beds of herbaceous plants and grasses, designed by horticulturalist Alan Bloom, are also now well established.

The Rose Garden is divided into modern cultivars and species, shrubs, and old-fashioned roses. A Formal Garden reflects the history of the 500-year-old house, its central feature, inspired by Tudor knot gardens, planted with herbs for medicinal and culinary use. There are also impressive mixed double borders, showing how perennials, shrubs, bedding, and bulbs can be planted for year-round colour and interest.

The undoubted star, however, is the 60-metre (200ft) herbaceous border, designed by Havergal, which flowers in three phases from late May until the frosts, starting with lupins, geraniums, and veronicas, then delphiniums, verbascum, and phlox. Concluding with late-flowering herbaceous plants like heleniums, rudbeckias, and asters, this outstanding display provides a glimpse into the garden's rich history.

Top *The herbaceous border, one of the finest in Britain, is at its best from late summer to autumn.*

Bottom *In the Formal Garden, neat hedging is softened by swathes of sage.*

FOCUS ON

Beatrix Havergal

Remembered for her pursuit of perfection in horticulture and as a pioneer in women's education, Beatrix Havergal (1901–1980) was a brilliant practical gardener and natural teacher. She set high standards for both staff and students, and the horticultural diploma she developed was considered on a par with that of Kew Gardens. Waterperry alumni include Pamela Schwerdt and Sibylle Kreutzberger, former head gardeners at Sissinghurst (see page 86).

Jellicoe & Aga Khan Gardens

WHERE *Coal Drops Yard, 5 Lewis Cubitt Walk, London, N1C 4DF* WHEN *All year round for design, structure, and planting* WHAT *Contemporary urban gardens, showing the influences of climate and culture from around the Islamic world*

Forming an integral part of the spectacular regeneration of London's bustling King's Cross area in recent years are two unexpected oases: the Jellicoe Gardens and the Islamic Gardens at the Aga Khan Centre. Both bring Persian-inspired beauty and tranquillity to hectic urban spaces.

The two gardens approach their inspiration from different perspectives. The Jellicoe Gardens manifest the design aesthetic of an Islamic paradise garden, with a twist, while the Aga Khan gardens demonstrate the diversity of gardens throughout the Muslim world.

AGA KHAN GARDENS

The six "hanging" gardens on different levels of the ten-storey Aga Khan Centre are pared-back, contemplative, contemporary spaces that embody many of the common features of Islamic garden design. The Terrace of Learning is influenced by the cloisters and courtyards of North Africa and southern Spain, while the Garden of Tranquillity is inspired by the loggias of Persia, Egypt, and the Middle East.

On the roof are three gardens, including the Garden of Life, inspired by the Mughal gardens of Central and South East Asia. This area is designed around the classic *charbagh* layout, where the garden is divided into four, with a water rill down its centre and fruit trees, including medlar, quince, and hazelnut, providing calming green softness.

THE JELLICOE GARDENS

A tribute to renowned architect, garden designer, and local resident Sir Geoffrey Jellicoe, these gardens, designed by Tom Stuart-Smith Studio, are based on the iconic sixteenth-century gardens at Bagh-e Fin in Iran, with the planting an English interpretation of the Islamic *bustan*, or fragrant orchard. Here, trees are underplanted with a meadow-like display of scented flowers. Colour-, texture-, and nectar-rich planting create an attractive, year-round wildlife habitat.

The upper garden, with its stainless-steel tubular pavilion, is fronted by a bubbling water feature, which feeds rills and pools. Oriental plane trees underplanted with evergreen shrubs *Osmanthus* and *Nandina* make the pavilion seem enclosed, while blue and white flowers – the colours of heaven – provide seasonal interest.

In the lower garden, seats are shaded by *Parrotia persica*, while beds are planted for year-round interest around evergreens that thrive in Mediterranean climates. Grasses are interwoven with bulbs and herbaceous plants to create a Persian carpet of soft pinks, reds, and blues.

Top *A traditional Islamic rill forms the spine of the Jellicoe Gardens, echoing the charbagh layout.*

Bottom *Garden of Light at the Aga Khan Centre, planted with* Magnolia × loebneri *'Merrill'.*

FOCUS ON

Geoffrey Jellicoe

Sir Geoffrey Jellicoe (1900–1996) was a town planner, architect, and landscape architect, who made an extensive study of Renaissance gardens, but he was also influenced by the artist Paul Klee, and later became interested in modern design. Water was a major element in some of his most successful schemes, including Shute House near Shaftsbury and the Water Gardens in Hemel Hempstead. Planting designs were often created by his wife, Susan, also a landscape architect.

Top *The turf amphitheatre, designed by Charles Bridgeman in the eighteenth century and restored in the 1970s, offers sweeping lake views.*

Bottom *Recent improvements have opened up vistas to John Vanbrugh's impressive Belvedere, which crowns the site on the Mount.*

FOCUS ON

The English Landscape Garden

This style of garden rejected earlier, French-influenced fashions for formality and order, instead arranging features to emphasize the landscape for a more natural, pastoral look, which was popular from the late seventeenth century. Features found in these gardens included vistas, serpentine lakes, classically styled temples, and rustic buildings.

Claremont Landscape Garden

WHERE *Esher, Surrey, KT10 9JG* WHEN *All year round* WHAT *Enduring eighteenth- and nineteenth-century landscape garden with a host of fascinating, carefully restored period features*

With owners that included a prime minister and royalty, Claremont is one of the earliest surviving examples of the English landscape garden and charts 300 years of horticultural history. Restoration continues, but its 20 hectares (49 acres) still display the original layout.

Just outside the commuter-belt town of Esher lies Claremont, a once-impressive estate that served as a retreat for a succession of influential owners. The Palladian mansion became a private school in 1930 when the wider estate was developed, while the landscape garden became overgrown, its features all but lost. However, after being passed to the National Trust, Claremont has been gradually restored. Today, it is the perfect place to learn about the evolution of eighteenth-century gardens.

LIVING GARDEN HISTORY

Claremont has an impressive pedigree. The estate was bought in 1709 by architect Sir John Vanbrugh but then sold to the Duke of Newcastle – who served twice as prime minister and, with Vanbrugh's help, transformed the house and garden. The most striking survivor from this era is the Belvedere. Designed by Vanbrugh and originally white, it sits atop the Mount as an imposing focal point. Owned by the school, it is open on occasional days and offers superb views across Surrey.

Much of the garden was set out for the duke by designer Charles Bridgeman in the 1720s. He created the Bowling Green with its avenue of beech hedges up to the Belvedere and, what has become Claremont's defining feature: the 1.2-hectare (3-acre) turf amphitheatre – the largest of its kind in Europe.

Just below is the lake. Originally, circular enlargements by landscape architect William Kent resulted in an irregular form. He also replaced a peacock-topped stone obelisk on the island with the handsome Belisle Pavilion, and constructed the grotto, now restored.

Ideally, choose a quiet weekday to visit, as Claremont is popular. In spring it is resplendent with daffodils and the old camellias on the terrace; in early summer rhododendrons provide colour; autumn is also superb with fiery tints of *Acer* and *Liquidambar*.

Paths weave through the vast Oudolf Landscape, with its rich carpet of 36,000 perennials, towards the Glasshouse.

RHS Garden Wisley

WHERE *Wisley Lane, Woking, Surrey* WHEN *An all-seasons garden, with an annual late-summer flower show* WHAT *The RHS's flagship garden, housing one of the largest plant collections in the world and demonstrating best horticultural practice*

From its origins as a 24-hectare (60-acre) experimental woodland garden, RHS Wisley has expanded both in size and ambition, and offers visitors an inspiring tour of the range of plants and landscapes that we could enjoy in our own gardens.

Wisley's now 97 hectares (240 acres) offer an astonishing 34 different areas of interest, from enclosed garden rooms to diverse woodland areas, a pinetum, arboretum, and orchards; from formal pools and fountains to wildlife ponds and lakes; from steep slopes and a viewing mount to flat expanses of lawn and flower meadows. That's before you arrive at the dedicated orchid house and the Glasshouse with its three climatic zones – tropical, moist temperate, and dry temperate – home to Wisley's tender plant collection. No wonder visitors are furnished with a free map on arrival, to help navigate around the dizzying diversity of its world-class plant collection, which thrives in often challenging conditions. Wisley endures frost pockets in winter and some of the highest temperatures in the South of England in summer.

Wisley is home to some 18 Plant Heritage National Plant Collections, and those interested in specialist plant groups might head straight for the Bowes-Lyon Rose Garden, where bulbs, perennials, and shrubs are interplanted with a selection of repeat-flowering roses. They might seek out the Alpine Houses, with their outdoor crevice garden, or the Heather Landscape where more than 900 different cultivars create ribbons of contrasting colours among yuccas and globe artichokes. Gardeners looking for practical information might prioritize the Trials Garden or the displays of plants given the Award of Garden Merit (AGM), while others may prefer to immerse themselves in colour, scent, foliage, and form as they wander from area to area, through the Cottage Garden, the Exotic Garden, the South African Meadow, and more.

LONG-FLOWERING MARVELS

The spectacle of one of Wisley's horticultural showstoppers, the 128-metre- (420ft-) long Mixed Borders, is achieved by a backbone of shrubs and trees, judicious staking, and early-season chopping to prolong flowering. Across the nearby Alpine Meadow, spangled with a

Clockwise from top

Clipped beech cylinders are offset by frothy Miscanthus *in the Glasshouse Landscape.*

Tresses of wisteria in bloom beside the Walled Garden, with the Old Laboratory behind.

Alpines, dwarf conifers, acers, and Japanese larch blend in the Rock Garden, which dates back to 1910.

> "Wisley is paramount to the history and progress of horticulture."
>
> GUY BARTER, RHS CHIEF HORTICULTURAL ADVISOR

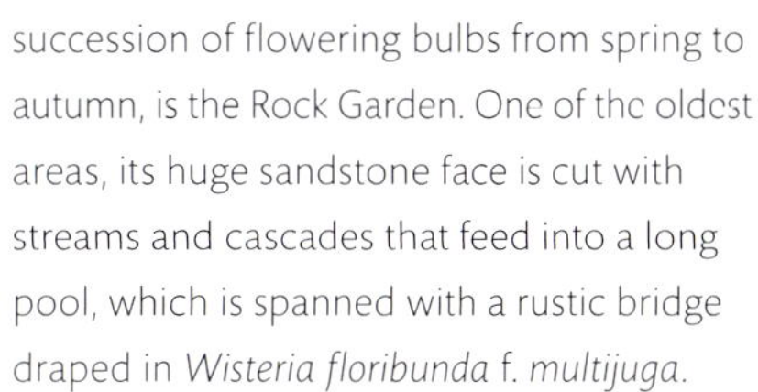

succession of flowering bulbs from spring to autumn, is the Rock Garden. One of the oldest areas, its huge sandstone face is cut with streams and cascades that feed into a long pool, which is spanned with a rustic bridge draped in *Wisteria floribunda* f. *multijuga*.

The garden has continued to evolve as changing conditions require new priorities. The destructive storm of 1987 decimated the Scots pines on the south-facing slopes of Battleston Hill, in turn creating the opportunity to make the Mediterranean Terraces, where succulents and cacti thrive in the sandy soil alongside loquats and mimosas. In 2021, with the opening of the sleek RHS Hilltop: The Home of Gardening Science building, three contemporary gardens were revealed: the Wellbeing Garden, the World Food Garden, and the Wildlife Garden – each providing inspiration for many kinds of gardeners.

FUTURE-PROOFING

A commitment to increasing biodiversity in the garden is exemplified in the redesigned Oudolf Landscape, by Dutch designer Piet Oudolf (see page 110). Here, some 36,000 perennials and grasses were planted in a network of meandering beds that invite visitors to lose themselves in the planting. This landscape is designed to survive with no additional watering once the plants are established, and the addition of a new irrigation lake, with a capacity of 9 million litres (2 million gallons) for periods of drought, is part of the RHS's strategy to be water neutral by 2030.

FOCUS ON

Wildlife Gardening

Ann-Marie Powell's Wildlife Garden, RHS Wisley's first garden specifically designed with wildlife in mind, is a tapestry of colourful flowers, both native and non-native, for much of the year, making it a magnet for pollinating insects and other bugs. It also shows that making a pond – whether small or large – and planting it with a range of floating and marginal plants, is one of the best ways to attract wildlife.

Left *The power station acts as a borrowed landscape for Jarman's industrial sculptures.*

Below *Self-seeded poppies weave the garden into its shingle surroundings.*

Bottom *Tough shrubs are trimmed by harsh weather into low, dense, mounds.*

GARDEN INSPIRATION

Push Boundaries

The garden is a place for self-expression. You don't have to follow trends; you can create them instead. You wouldn't expect to find foxgloves growing on a shingle beach, but in this garden they do, very happily. Work with your surroundings and don't be afraid to experiment.

Derek Jarman's Garden

WHERE *Dungeness, Romney Marsh, Kent, TN29 9NE* WHEN *May to July when the garden is in bloom; year-round for sculpture and structure* WHAT *The garden as art, with organic sculpture and salt- and drought-tolerant plantings*

Derek Jarman – artist, film-maker, gay rights activist, and gardener – bought derelict Prospect Cottage in 1984 and in eight short years, although burdened by illness, transformed the surrounding space into an iconic, postmodern, contextually sensitive garden of extremes.

Derek Jarman regularly returned home from his forays along Dungeness Beach with flotsam and jetsam, ranging from seaworn timbers and artistic, rusting metal to small spanners, chains, and twisted metal. Fascinated by magic and alchemy, he also collected rounded flints, or "dragon's teeth", which were placed to mimic neolithic standing stones and create patterns in the shingle. Jarman did not initially intend to create a garden but realized over time that, in placing these objects, he had created the structure of one.

THE RESILIENCE OF PLANTS

The first planting, a dog rose (*Rosa canina*) that Jarman found along the beach, was marked by a driftwood stake hung with a necklace of stones. Other plants were gifted, bought from nurseries, or self-seeded, often originating in Mediterranean climates due to their tolerance of salt, heat, drought, and battering winds.

Jarman regarded his garden as a pharmacopoeia, full of medicinal and culinary plants, and there is a mix of low-growing shrubs, perennials, biennials, and annuals. Endemics include sea kale (the largest population in Britain is found on Dungeness Beach); green spiny mounds of gorse, which is perpetually in bright-yellow flower; golden-yellow horned poppies; pink-purple foxgloves; teasels; blue viper's bugloss; red field poppies; and bright-orange California poppies. Cotton lavender, rock roses, rue, and irises also thrive in these conditions. There are unusual plants like the monocarpic *Angelica pachycarpa* – a gift from Christopher Lloyd (see page 84), who, along with Beth Chatto (see page 62), became a close friend. After an experiment to grow leafy vegetables failed, the raised beds have now been restored and are used as trial beds, particularly for ornamental *Phlomis*.

After Jarman's death, his partner, Keith Collins, lovingly tended the garden for 25 years, and although it declined during his final illness the garden was revived under the hand of their mutual friend and gardener Jonny Bruce. In 2020, after a £3.5 million fundraising campaign, Prospect Cottage was bought for the nation.

The Peacock Garden, created by Nathanial Lloyd, is now a place of fantastic contrast, where bird topiary rubs shoulders with a carefree blend of ferula, gladioli, and euphorbia.

Great Dixter

WHERE *Northiam, Rye, East Sussex, TN31 6PH* WHEN *From late spring until early autumn*
WHAT *An Arts and Crafts layout with adventurous, ever-evolving planting*

Once the home of writer-gardener Christopher Lloyd, Great Dixter blends innovation with tradition. Exciting plant combinations change year on year within a semi-formal layout set beside wildflower-filled meadows. It never stands still, always surprises, and excels in biodiversity.

Great Dixter is one of the world's best-loved gardens, famed for its exuberant, experimental plantings, which set trends and inspire gardeners worldwide. Christopher Lloyd's father, Nathanial, bought Great Dixter in 1910, and employed architect Edwin Lutyens to transform it into a family home. Meadows originally ran up to the house, but Lloyd and Lutyens also set out a garden, divided by walls and yew hedges – a novel concept at the time.

Today the garden's character varies hugely; in some years it feels fairly restrained, in others it is wild and free. The effect can leave visitors feeling child-like, immersed in planting as they weave through. The change from season to season is just as profound, the successional planting a masterclass. Early bulbs are followed by spring-flowering perennials, which, as they fade, are hidden by bold summer foliage.

TRADITION AND INNOVATION

The house, with its characterful leaning porch, is approached from the Front Meadow, which in May is resplendent with blue camassias, native orchids, and golden buttercups. To one side are the Barn and Sunk Gardens, to the other the Peacock Garden, with bird topiary created by Nathanial Lloyd, and beyond, the High Garden, its overflowing borders backed with ancient espalier fruit trees. The back of the house is more open, with the Topiary Lawn – now a flowery meadow – and the famed Long Border, stretching for 100 metres (328ft).

Down the Circular Steps (often bedded with cacti and succulents) is one of the most talked-about areas: the Old Rose Garden. Here, in 1993, Christopher Lloyd and head gardener Fergus Garrett replaced roses with a jungle of exotic cannas, bananas, papyrus, and dahlias, sparking controversy and a new craze. Today you'll also find palms, tree ferns, and conifers.

As well as exotics, Christopher Lloyd was also interested in wildlife, and gardened accordingly. Meadow cutting is delayed until insect activity has slowed and seeds are set, while seedheads are left for the birds. In 2019, a biodiversity audit revealed that Dixter supports an abundance of life as rich as many nature reserves – 2,029 species recorded – once again inspiring gardeners to do things differently.

Irises line the water's edge of the medieval moat, which forms part of the garden boundary.

Sissinghurst Castle Garden

WHERE *Sissinghurst, Cranbrook, Kent, TN17 2AB* WHEN *Year-round interest*
WHAT *The romantic garden created by Vita Sackville-West and Harold Nicolson, which has been kept true to its spirit by successive National Trust head gardeners*

This 2.4-hectare (6-acre) garden laid out as a series of rooms around the ruins of an Elizabethan manor is arguably one of the most influential gardens in the world, thanks to its creators' relaxed, romantic planting within a strong framework of hedges, walls, and walkways.

The entrance to Sissinghurst's garden is through an archway in what remains of the historic manor house to a grass courtyard where four sentinel Irish yews lead the eye to the sixteenth-century twin-turreted Tower, the evocative centrepiece of the garden. It is here that writer and poet Vita Sackville-West had her writing room, with a view across the garden she created with her husband, the diplomat and journalist Harold Nicolson.

Today, a climb to the roof not only rewards the visitor with a bird's-eye view of the interconnecting garden rooms, but also of the Kentish farmland that surrounds it. The garden was developed as themed rooms around a collection of buildings where the couple lived with their two sons, and beyond to the open expanses of the Orchard, the Moat, and the Nuttery – a planting of coppiced Kentish cobnuts lush with ferns in summer.

GARDEN ROOMS

The garden rooms and walkways are defined by a framework of clipped yew hedges and brick walls, which Vita planted with an array of climbers, especially her beloved roses. Archways and gateways in the walls and hedges open up views and provide links between the rooms, several of which are colour themed.

On one side of the grass courtyard is the White Garden, one of the most-copied planting schemes of the garden, which shows Vita's

inspired use of grey, green, and silver foliage plants, which create foils for a sea of white blooms from the trumpets of *Lilium regale* to the spires of eremurus, foxgloves, delphiniums, and galtonias. On the southern side of the courtyard is Sissinghurst's famous Rose Garden, which Vita filled with fragrant old shrub roses, combining them with a selection of perennials and bulbs in soft colours, including irises, peonies, violas, pinks, and alliums. In contrast, the adjoining Cottage Garden, which Harold overlooked from his study in the South Cottage, is awash with shades of red, yellow, and orange from a mixture of traditional cottage-garden plants such as potentillas, irises, and wallflowers, and tender exotics such as cannas.

Harold's special garden was the pleached Lime Walk, connecting the Nuttery with the Rose Garden, which he designed and underplanted with a springtime display of bulbs and primroses. Beyond the Nuttery is the tranquil herb garden, hidden behind buttressed yew hedging. The centrepiece is a shallow stone dish, supported by a trio of lions, and currently planted with succulents. This delightful planter, purchased by Harold when he lived in Constantinople, is a reminder that this is, at heart, a richly personal garden.

It's a garden that also looks ahead. Under head gardener Troy Scott Smith, Sissinghurst is embracing waterwise gardening. In summer, watering is now restricted to new plantings and pots, and the team is looking at how to harvest rainwater from the buildings for this purpose. Hardy annuals are now sown in October and planted out in February (instead of May), when they can establish without extra irrigation.

FOCUS ON

Delos

After Vita and Harold visited the Greek island of Delos, where wildflowers grew profusely over rocky terraces, they made their own Delos at Sissinghurst. However, the north-facing garden, behind the Priest's House, was not a success. In 2019 shade-casting trees were removed and new terracing constructed that leans south to capture maximum light. Some 6,000 plants native to the Mediterranean basin now flourish there in gritty, nutrient-poor soil.

Top *The view across the orchard, which is studded with a succession of bulbs, to the Elizabethan Tower.*

Bottom Rosa *'Mulliganii' covers the ironwork bower in the White Garden, amid spires of eremurus, foxgloves, and delphiniums.*

TIMELINE OF EVENTS

1570s

Sissinghurst's Elizabethan manor house, built on the site of a Saxon pig farm, acquires a twin-turreted tower as a grand gateway.

1756–63

The house is used as a prisoner-of-war camp in the Seven Years' War.

1796–1855

The estate is leased to the parish as a poor house where around 100 men work the farm. It later reverts to the Mann-Cornwallis family.

1930

Vita Sackville-West and Harold Nicolson buy the estate. They clear the site, lay out their garden, and by 1950 it has become a working farm again.

1962

Vita Sackville-West dies, and Sissinghurst becomes a National Trust property.

Left *Neat as a pin and highly productive, the Kitchen Garden has an unusual oval shape.*

Below *Dahlias,* Tagetes *'Cinnabar', and cannas add hot notes to a mixed border designed by head gardener Tom Coward.*

GARDEN INSPIRATION

Versatile Vegetables

Robinson believed that by growing vegetables intensively and on flat-roofed houses, more people, particularly the poor, could be fed. You can embrace this idea by growing vegetables, fruit, and herbs among flowers, in window boxes, in pots and recycled containers, in grow bags – anything, provided it has drainage holes. Crops can also be grown vertically or up walls, as long as they can be safely reached for maintenance and harvest.

Gravetye Manor

WHERE *West Hoathly, East Sussex, RH19 4LJ* WHEN *Year-round interest in the ornamental and Kitchen Garden; spring blossom in the Orchards; spring to autumn in the Meadows* WHAT *A historic garden, once home to free-thinking writer and gardener William Robinson*

The 12-hectare (30-acre) garden that surrounds the sixteenth-century Gravetye Manor House, now a hotel, was developed by renowned gardener William Robinson, pioneer of the English natural style, from 1885 until his death in 1935. This ever-changing garden is undergoing a complete restoration in the Robinsonian style.

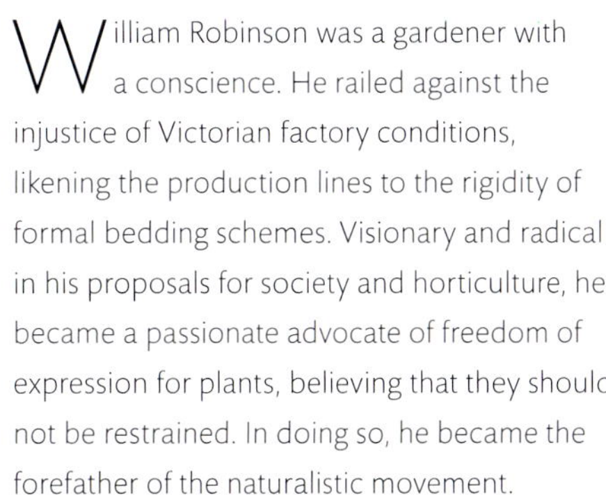

William Robinson was a gardener with a conscience. He railed against the injustice of Victorian factory conditions, likening the production lines to the rigidity of formal bedding schemes. Visionary and radical in his proposals for society and horticulture, he became a passionate advocate of freedom of expression for plants, believing that they should not be restrained. In doing so, he became the forefather of the naturalistic movement.

He expounded his ideas in his own journals and books, including *The Wild Garden* (1870) and *The English Flower Garden* (1883). The success of these publications and his shrewd business acumen brought him great wealth, and on moving into Gravetye Manor in 1885, he began his experiments in naturalistic gardening, which still characterize the garden today.

ROBINSON REVISITED

In the Flower Garden, spring begins with a display of tulips, followed by multi-layered successional plantings of annuals and tender perennials, mixed with herbaceous perennials and shrubs, creating a pleasing and ever-changing display until the first frosts. Campanulas, foxgloves, and sweet rocket are followed by the colourful spikes of shrubby salvias and lupins, while tender annuals and self-sowers fill the gaps. Shrubs provide permanent structure and a framework for late-flowering climbers. Robinson, who developed the idea of mixed borders, would be delighted by the relaxed, experimental planting at Gravetye today.

The unique, elliptical walled Kitchen Garden on a south-facing slope, which was begun in 1898 and took three years to build, captures light and warmth, creating optimum growing conditions for the finest fruit and vegetables for the hotel's Michelin-starred restaurant, while some of the trees in the 0.8-hectare (2-acre) Orchards date back to Robinson's day.

Robinson championed the ornamental use of meadows, and the 2.4-hectare (6-acre) examples at Gravetye perfectly encapsulate his ideas. In late winter and early spring, snowdrops and crocuses are followed by daffodils, scilla, species tulips, and camassias. Later in the year, the Meadows are filled with native wildflowers blooming from May until September. A man ahead of his time, Robinson's influence among gardeners remains as strong as ever.

Borde Hill

WHERE *Borde Hill, Haywards Heath, West Sussex, RH16 1XP* WHEN *Spring for flowering trees; summer for herbaceous highlights; autumn for woodland fiery shades* WHAT *A heritage garden set in 155 hectares (383 acres) of parkland, renowned for its rare trees and shrubs, and enhanced with a succession of recent plantings*

Five generations of the Stephenson Clarke family have created this delightful garden, which boasts one of the rarest trees in the world, some 70 champion trees, and contemporary herbaceous planting.

The bones of this 17-hectare (42-acre) garden were laid out in Edwardian times by plantsman and plant collector extraordinaire Colonel Stephenson Robert Clarke, and it is thanks to his vision that visitors now can immerse themselves in banks of towering rhododendrons, lofty magnolias, blazing azaleas, and various rare and beautiful trees from around the world.

In some parts, such as the Long Dell, where a former quarry is lush with trees and shrubs from China, it is easy to imagine you are in a Himalayan landscape. In the woods, oak, hazel, and beech provide shelter for some of the earliest introductions, including one of the rarest trees in the world, *Meliosma alba*, which produces panicles of creamy flowers in May.

FLOWER GARDENS

With the additions made by subsequent generations of the family, there are now a series of flower gardens to enjoy as well. These include a formal Italian Garden on two levels, with a reflecting pool framed by topiary, parterre beds, and large clay pots; Jay Robin's Rose Garden, with more than 750 fragrant roses in colour-themed arrangements, and a Round Dell filled with subtropical plants, which have been augmented, in a design by Sophie Walker, with species grown by modern-day plant hunters Bleddyn and Sue Wynn-Jones. You will also find the long border along the Paradise Walk, redesigned by Chris Beardshaw, who selected 70 different perennials for scent and colour in shades of blue, lilac, cream, and pale yellow to provide interest from spring to late autumn.

SPRING SPECTACULAR

Many of the garden's original tree and shrub plantings are magnificent in spring, especially in the Azalea Ring, a horseshoe-shaped collection of azaleas in white, yellow, orange, pink, and crimson. It is here that Borde Hill's iconic tree *Emmenopterys henryi*, grown from seed collected in China by George Forrest, was planted in 1928, producing its fragrant white flowers for the first time 83 years later.

Clockwise from right
Knap Hill and Ghent azaleas sit happily with hostas in the Azalea Ring.

Jay Robin's Rose Garden sits against a contrasting backdrop of yew hedging.

The unusual creamy flowers of Emmenopterys henryi*, planted in 1928.*

FOCUS ON

Champion Trees

Champion trees are those listed on the Tree Register as being the biggest by girth and/or height in the British Isles, and Borde Hill has some 70 – thought to be the largest number in a private collection. The woodland glade has sandy soil, which suited many of the garden's introductions from China and Burma, including three champion magnolias planted in the 1930s, and plant collector E.H. Wilson's *Liriodendron chinense*, the first specimen to flower outside China, in 1927.

Fastigiate hornbeams bisect the prairie borders where grasses create rhythm and movement through the perennials.

Sussex Prairies Wild

WHERE *Henfield, West Sussex, BN5 9AT* WHEN *Open by appointment to groups, June to October; at its most statuesque in late summer* WHAT *A tapestry of prairie-style perennials and grasses planted on a vast scale*

From midsummer until late autumn, this large Sussex garden is an exciting place to explore prairie-style planting at ground level, along grass and woodchip paths, and from above in the RIBA award-winning Viewing Tower, designed by Sandy Rendel Architects.

This 3-hectare (8-acre) garden on the site of an agricultural field started as a series of plans drawn up in the winter of 2007 by owners Pauline and Paul McBride. With help, they planted some 30,000 perennials, grasses, and bulbs in arc-shaped beds that trace the spirals of a nautilus shell. Two years later, planting was sufficiently established for them to welcome visitors into what is now one of the UK's largest and most exciting prairie gardens, featuring around 60,000 plants and 1,600 varieties.

The McBrides were inspired by the naturalistic planting style of Piet Oudolf (see page 110), planting large drifts of single varieties (rudbeckias, for example, are planted in groups of up to 1,500) and creating a garden with remarkable impact – and at a fraction of the cost of a shrub-and-tree scheme.

PLANT CHOICE

Bark-chip paths that snake through the wide beds enable the McBrides to access the plants while also allowing visitors to immerse themselves in the planting, which by the end of the summer can soar and sway at head height, with grasses such as *Calamagrostis × acutiflora* 'Karl Foerster' and *Stipa gigantea*, and perennials such as *Eupatorium* and *Vernonia arkansana* 'Mammuth'. Their choice of plants, which includes many unusual varieties, is based on shape, flower colour, and long-season interest, as well as ease of propagation. Plants also need to make good companions, so that each variety benefits from enough light and root space.

As the season progresses the colour palette becomes more fiery, with bands of kniphofias, heleniums, and cannas lighting up the borders. Massed plantings of *Miscanthus sinensis* 'Kleine Silberspinne' create a river of silky plumes down the central path, where a line of steel buffaloes is a playful reminder that many of these plants originate in the plains of North America.

In the former cutting garden, the McBrides are tackling climate change by experimenting with plants that do better with low summer rainfall, such as amsonias and nepeta. They are also embracing a less managed regime for the borders where more native species and blow-ins will be welcomed, in line with their rewilding ambitions for the whole farm.

Denmans Garden

WHERE *Fontwell, Sussex, BN18 0SU* WHEN *An all-seasons garden, but it is particularly special in winter* WHAT *A Grade II listed contemporary country garden reshaped by landscape designer John Brookes*

This 1.6-hectare (4-acre) country garden is both a plant lover's haven and a lesson in contemporary garden design, thanks to the hands-on involvement of its two owners, horticulturalist Joyce Robinson and, from 1980 to 2018, landscape designer, teacher, and author John Brookes, when it became his home.

When John Brookes first visited Denmans in 1973, he fell in love with its naturalistic style, its intimacy and tranquillity. He was also fascinated by owner Joyce Robinson's use of gravel as a planting medium.

When he moved into the former stable block in 1980 and took over the management of the garden, he was determined to retain the special atmosphere and rich mix of plants but felt the garden needed to flow better, so set about connecting the various parts with curvilinear borders and paths. He also added strong evergreen structure, ponds, and sculpture.

MAKING CONNECTIONS

The garden extends on either side of the Gardener's Cottage where Joyce Robinson lived. The main part was conceived as a series of densely planted beds, grass and gravel walkways, a flowery meadow, an orchard, a walled garden, two glasshouses, and, flowing across and down the garden, two gravel riverbeds, created by Robinson, who was inspired by local rivers that run dry in summer. Each "river" is planted with a mix of sun-loving plants, including irises and aquilegias for spring and asters, kniphofias, and sedums for later in summer, with self-seeders such as *Verbascum bombyciferum* adding to the naturalistic effect.

A ROOM OUTSIDE

In 1970 the first gravel beds were laid out in the Walled Garden. Perennials, herbs, and annuals self-seed in the gravel, while the borders are filled with a profusion of shrubs and perennials, including roses, wisteria, pomegranate, kiwis, and myrtle. Brookes added architectural plants, box topiary, and his iconic blue benches, lending this part of the garden a Mediterranean feel.

Behind the Gardener's Cottage is the garden John Brookes designed. Here, flowing shapes have been swapped for rectilinear gravel beds and box cubes. The planting, which includes phormiums, Chusan palms, and *Echium vulgare*, has a subtropical feel. A pergola attached to the house provides a semi-shaded seating area, and creates a "Room Outside", a feature that Brookes introduced to a generation of designers.

Kniphofias, asters, and geraniums grow naturalistically against architectural plants in the Walled Garden.

Left *Clematis and roses cascade over the elegant Edwardian pergola.*

Below *Wall-trained apple and pear trees are both productive and stylish in the Kitchen Garden.*

Bottom *In the beautiful walled gardens, many traditional horticultural methods are still in use.*

FOCUS ON

West Dean's Glasshouses

The 13 greenhouses within the walled gardens of West Dean date from between 1890 and 1900. Originally built by the firm Foster & Pearson, all were restored in the early 1990s. Among them, you will find a fig house, peach house, melon house, tropical houses, propagation houses, and a vinery. During the year collections of tomatoes, florist's ranunculus, pelargoniums, gourds, and nerines are grown in these impressive structures.

West Dean Gardens

WHERE *Chichester, West Sussex, PO18 0QZ* WHEN *Year-round interest*
WHAT *The gardens of West Dean House, including an extensive restored Victorian walled garden featuring a range of working glasshouses*

A visit to West Dean can transport you back to the glory days of horticulture. Experience the walled gardens with 13 plant-filled glasshouses, and the superb Edwardian pergola cascading with climbers. Recent changes, however, also make this garden fit for the future.

Considered one of the greatest restored gardens in England, West Dean is best known for its walled gardens – probably the closest we can now get to experiencing a traditional productive garden. We have husband-and-wife team Jim Buckland and Sarah Wain to thank; they led West Dean through years of restoration, a legacy ably continued by current head gardener Tom Brown, who is taking the gardens into exciting – and sustainable – new directions.

Be it the greenhouses and hot beds filled with exotic plants and crops, the impressive Fruit Garden, the Kitchen Garden, or the Cutting Garden, the productive gardens are the heart of the site. In spring, greenhouses overflow with developing plants. In summer visitors can marvel at the subtropical border, sumptuous grapes in the Vinery, and fuchsia displays. In autumn, see crops of orchard fruit, pumpkins, and fiery chillies, In winter enjoy displays in the Tropical House.

OLD AND NEW

West Dean's famous pergola must surely rank among the finest anywhere. This Edwardian beauty was designed by architect and designer Harold Peto. It runs 100 metres (300ft) east to west across the North Lawn, with Italianate stone pillars supporting oak crossbeams and domes, up which wisteria, clematis, and climbing roses are beautifully trained. Internal beds feature shade-loving ferns and hostas, while outside south-facing borders shimmer with bearded irises, roses, and salvias.

To the east lies a waterlily-filled pool and, beyond it, the restored and expanded Sunken Garden. This superb area complements the pergola perfectly, with bulbs and low-growing plants cascading over the walls. Recent changes include a thyme lawn and replacement of pest-and-disease-prone box hedging.

A fascinating new area is the Dry Meadow Garden, an experimental scheme in response to increasingly hot, dry summers. Here, the ground is mulched with broken recycled concrete to hold in moisture, and planted with deep-rooted, drought-tolerant perennials such as *Eryngium*, *Agastache*, *Verbascum*, and *Berkheya* in a naturalistically styled blend. Don't miss the Spring Garden with its riverside plantings and bridges, and, further afield, the Arboretum – well worth the 2.5-mile (4km) circular walk.

Sir Harold Hillier Gardens

WHERE *Ampfield, nr Romsey, Hampshire, SO51 0QA* WHEN *All year round*
WHAT *An expansive garden and arboretum featuring important collections of trees and shrubs*

If you enjoy admiring the finest cultivated plants, these world-renowned gardens covering some 73 hectares (180 acres) are an unmissable treat. Wander through the Himalayan Valley, marvel at spring displays or enjoy the fragrance of spidery witch hazels in the Winter Garden.

Known to many simply as "Hillier's", this much-loved garden was started in the 1950s by nurseryman Sir Harold Hillier in the grounds around his home, Jermyn's House. His expertise is immediately clear, as one of the first plantings visitors encounter is the National Collection Glade. Spread through the gardens are a remarkable 14 National Plant Collections, including *Cornus*, *Hypericum*, *Pinus*, and *Quercus*.

There is also an exceptional number of champion trees (in excess of 600) to see, many the result of Sir Harold's early plantings. In the Rhododendron Woodland, for example, stands an impressive *Quercus rysophylla*, a Mexican oak collected by Harold on one of his expeditions. Another specimen, *Metasequoia glyptostroboides* (dawn redwood), was raised from the original batch of seed sent from China in 1948.

Perhaps the best-known area is the sheltered Himalayan Valley behind Jermyn's House, with fine collections of ericaceous plants. A shaded path leads to the lush Bog Garden with its vast bamboos and bright displays of candelabra primulas. Beyond this lies the Pond, where examples of swamp cypress tower, their feathery foliage glowing bronze-red before falling in autumn. In spring, Magnolia Avenue in front of the house is spectacular, as is Spring Walk, with its colourful camellias and rhododendrons.

BRANCHING OUT

In recent years the garden has successfully diversified. The remarkable Centenary Border stretches some 250 metres (820ft) – making it among the longest in the UK. Originally planted in the 1960s, it was redesigned from 2010 to 2013 with paved access paths and a circular lawned area in the middle. The planting now includes not only shrubs and roses, but also herbaceous perennials and grasses in dazzling combinations from spring to autumn.

At Hillier's, you'll also find one of the finest – and largest – winter gardens anywhere. It has everything, from *Betula*, *Cornus*, and *Salix*, to rare bamboos, to evergreen conifers, to the perfumed flowers of *Daphne*, *Hamamelis*, and *Sarcococca* and, blooming below, the first snowdrops and crocuses, all artfully combined.

Top *Golden oats stipa and pampas grass accent autumn tree colour beside the Pond.*

Bottom *Sunlight glimmers through golden bamboo and catches the leaves of shield ferns.*

TIMELINE OF EVENTS

1951

Sir Harold Hillier buys Jermyn's House.

1960s

Gardens expand as Sir Harold buys neighbouring properties.

1964–6

The Himalayan Valley is first planted.

1964

The Centenary Border is created.

1970s

The Pinetum is planted.

1977

Gardens become a charitable trust.

1997

Gurkha Memorial Garden is added.

1998

Winter Garden is opened.

2013

Redesigned Centenary Border opens.

2014

Winter Garden is extended.

2021

Himalayan Valley is revised.

In the Walled Garden, pink diascias and silver Stachys byzantina *spill into the path. Height is added by cardoons.*

Farringford

WHERE *Bedbury Lane, Freshwater Bay, Isle of Wight, PO40 9PE* WHEN *From April to October; June and July for old-fashioned scented roses* WHAT *A sensitively restored Victorian garden rich in history and poetry*

We have the garden and parkland of Farringford to thank for some the greatest works of the nineteenth-century poet Alfred, Lord Tennyson. Now, the heritage of his treasured and beautiful garden has been lovingly respected in its recent restoration.

One of the most famous poets of the Victorian era, Alfred, Lord Tennyson moved from London to the historic island property of Farringford in 1853, and it is from this residence that he produced some of his most notable poems. It was sold by the Tennyson family in 1945, then used as a hotel, but thanks to the meticulous restoration carried out by the current owner, the property and its gardens have been largely returned to their Victorian heyday and are now open to the public.

STARTING FROM SCRATCH

A keen gardener, Tennyson was passionate about plants. The restoration of his 0.8-hectare (2-acre) Walled Garden began in 2014 when the 18 self-catering bungalows that sat on the site were demolished. A visit to Farringford starts by walking through the revived Walled Garden, and in summer the scent of roses and sweet peas welcomes you. This cottage-style kitchen garden has now been replanted by gardeners Ellen and Alastair Penstone-Smith with fruit and vegetables, as well as ornamentals that are free to self-seed in among the edibles, as they did in Tennyson's day. "It's a once-in-a-lifetime opportunity for us to rebuild a garden from scratch," explains Ellen. "Putting the garden back from nothing has been a joy. It's such a lovely spot, and when you watch the sun setting over the horizon you can see why Tennyson loved it so much."

Contemporaneous descriptions of Tennyson's garden from his wife, Emily, in her journal entries, as well as the watercolours by Victorian illustrator Helen Allingham, have been used as references for the current garden team, and in just a few short years the garden has achieved horticultural excellence, receiving plenty of industry plaudits. Popular plants of the day such as roses, lilies, poppies, delphiniums, and nicotiana have been replanted, and an impressive hazel tunnel offers support to squashes and runner beans.

The wider parkland, offering glimpses of the sea across the downs and, if you're lucky, red squirrels, covers 13 hectares (32 acres). Work on this extensive area continues at a pace, with plans to reintroduce wildflowers and meadows that befit the poetry of the place.

TIMELINE OF EVENTS

1853

Alfred and Emily Tennyson rent Farringford.

1856

The Tennysons buy the property.

1945

The Tennyson family sells Farringford and it becomes a hotel.

2010

The hotel closes.

2012

Restoration of the house begins.

2014

Eighteen bungalows are demolished in the Walled Garden.

2016

Garden restoration starts; pool and golf course are returned to parkland.

2017

Garden is planted and opened to the public.

2024

Farringford is awarded Wight in Bloom overall winner and RHS Partner Garden of the Year.

Hidcote

WHERE *Hidcote Bartrim, Chipping Campden, Gloucestershire, GL55 6LR* WHEN *Year-round interest for plantings and colour; visit in winter to admire the bones of the garden* WHAT *A classic 4.2-hectare (10½-acre) Arts and Crafts-influenced garden, divided into themed rooms and spaces*

This most quintessentially English of gardens was designed and created by an American who was born in Paris, Lawrence Johnston, and it is now renowned worldwide. It is a garden full of design influences, but the creative genius was Johnston's own.

Major Lawrence Johnston possessed a diversity of talents rarely found in one person – architect, artist, gardener, and plant expert – and they all came together in his creation at Hidcote. Self-educated in horticulture and influenced by the Arts and Crafts movement, which celebrated the traditional hands-on craftsmanship seen in the walls, terraces, and gazebos of this garden, he added elements from other eras and cultures, too, including French and Italian gardens.

His mother, Gertrude, bought Hidcote Manor and its farmland estate in 1907, expecting her son to maintain an interest in farming, but as his fascination with horticulture took over, he expanded the existing garden into the farmland. Johnston created rooms and spaces on different themes – there is the White Garden, the Stilt Garden of pleached hornbeams, a Mediterranean-style garden, and the Wilderness – which became less formal further away from the house.

Most famously, Johnston mastered colour theming in his famous double Red Borders of blazing shrubs, annuals, and perennials. Since his day there has been a multitude of shades jostling for attention here, from crimson to vermillion, punctuated with soft-orange day lilies, rich-purple aconites, and dark dahlia foliage for balance and contrast. Intense, even overpowering, these borders were designed to be seen in passing, rather than when seated.

Johnston also incorporated breathing spaces into the garden, however, like the restful green of the Theatre Lawn and the Long Walk, with vistas that link the garden to the surrounding countryside and its "borrowed" views, notably from Heaven's Gate to the Malvern Hills beyond.

CURIOSITY REWARDED

There is no prescribed route around the garden. Creating your own inevitably breeds a frisson of excitement, with a reveal at every junction, corner, or entrance. Johnston was a master at using the momentum of curiosity to propel visitors around the site, encouraging them from space to vista to room, with different exits on offer within the gardens or sneak previews of what lies ahead. It is this, combined with Johnston's finely tuned sense of beauty, symmetry, and proportion, that makes a visit such a pleasurable adventure.

Clockwise from right

Aquilegias fill the borders of the Pillar Garden.

Frothy sprays of Crambe cordifolia *flower alongside lupins and foxgloves in the Long Borders.*

Pleached hornbeam trees define the formal space of the Stilt Garden.

FOCUS ON

Lavender

Lavandula angustifolia 'Hidcote' was selected by Johnston in the 1920s, probably from France, and named after his house and garden. Compact, hardy, and with beautiful deep-violet flower spires, it was given the Award of Garden Merit by the RHS in 1932, and by the late 1940s was a commercial success. It is now one of the most popular lavenders among growers in the UK.

Top *Autumn mist begins to lift from the Dragon Garden and its pool.*

Bottom *The silvery-pink flowers of* Pennisetum orientale *'Shogun'.*

GARDEN INSPIRATION

Pennisetums

Commonly (and aptly) known as fountain grass, *Pennisetum* is a diverse group. They range dramatically in height and are perfect for a pot or border. Plant in a well-drained, sunny spot where you can touch the soft, bottle-brush-style flowers.

Knoll Gardens

WHERE *Hampreston, Wimborne, Dorset, BH21 7ND* WHEN *At its best from late summer to late autumn, when the grasses are at their peak* WHAT *Wildlife-focused, meadow-style planting and renowned collections of ornamental grasses*

Knoll Gardens offers a masterclass in how to create a naturalistic garden that appeals as much to its visitors as it does to wildlife. Internationally acclaimed grass expert Neil Lucas has been welcoming both to the garden since 1994.

One visit to Knoll will win over anyone who is unsure about the value of ornamental grasses. Within the 1.6-hectare (4-acre) garden there is a gallery of grasses, from panicum, to miscanthus, to calamagrostis, to molinia, which demonstrates their year-round interest, their ease, and their appeal to wildlife. In the work of the Knoll Gardens Foundation, volunteers survey the wildlife that visits, to build a picture of how each area of the garden offers protection, habitat, and sustenance to butterflies, moths, and pollinating insects.

Knoll is also home to the National Plant Collection of *Pennisetum*, showcasing the varied growing environments enjoyed by each species. Under the care of Neil Lucas, this garden has put ornamental grasses on the map and clearly demonstrates their versatility.

A GARDEN FOR THE SENSES

A vast array of different grasses can be found in the distinct areas of Knoll where they are best suited to the conditions – in the Shady or Damp Garden, the Water Garden or Dry Meadow. The Gravel Garden is home to *Agapanthus* 'Northern Star', *Pennisetum macrourum*, and *Oenothera lindheimeri* 'Whirling Butterflies' – specimens that can be bought as well as admired in the adjoining nursery. With informal drifts interplanted with perennials and bulbs for colour, texture, and contrast, schemes are designed to be low maintenance, while delivering maximum impact and multi-season interest. The journey through the garden shows how grasses can also be used to screen or divide a space and lead you from one area to another.

The garden shines brightest in late summer and early autumn, when many of the grasses are in flower. The low summer sun dancing through the naturalistic planting creates an undeniably beautiful scene. The garden delights all the senses as the grasses sway elegantly in the breeze and in many cases are soft to the touch. Informal in design with winding paths and changes in level, Knoll offers a sense of adventure and escapism.

Top *Bold yew and box topiary takes inspiration from Italian gardens.*

Bottom *Porticoes create an elegant backdrop to the English-style planting on the Great Terrace.*

Iford Manor

WHERE *Bradford-on-Avon, Wiltshire, BA15 2BA* WHEN *Year-round interest*
WHAT *A masterfully designed hillside garden with terraces ornamented with Italian artefacts and garden buildings, taking in bucolic views of valley pastures and meadows*

This Grade I-listed garden, created by British architect and garden designer Harold Peto, represents a masterful fusion of Italian design principles and the quintessential English landscape.

Nestled at the bottom of the picturesque valley of the River Frome, the garden at Iford Manor was hewn from terrain that didn't lend itself to a conventional layout. Enter architect Harold Peto. He acquired the property in 1899 and it remained his home until his death in 1933; in that time he brought together his great love of classic Italian design and archetypal English planting, creating a tour de force in garden design and a garden that captivates at every turn of the path.

PERFECTLY PLACED

Peto's genius lay in creating a series of terraces that cascade down the hillside, each offering new discoveries within the garden, as well as borrowing views from the countryside beyond. At the heart of the design lies the Great Terrace, featuring a loggia adorned with columns, artefacts, and architectural fragments collected by Peto on his extensive travels. Throughout the garden, Peto carefully positioned these pieces to create spatial structure, and give a sense of historical continuity and architectural harmony.

From the Great Terrace run steps and paths connecting to other terraces and sections of the garden, each showcasing different aspects of the designer's philosophy. Examples are the Casita, which provides a sheltered spot for contemplation, and the Italian-style Cloister, constructed in 1914, where ancient architectural fragments create an atmosphere of timeless tranquillity. The cloisters and terraces are also adorned with classical statuary, including a prominent statue of Britannia that has stood in its position for over a century.

Peto was heavily influenced by William Robinson's naturalistic style (see page 90) as well as the Arts and Crafts movement (see page 28), using informal planting to complement the strong use of architecture. Mediterranean feature specimens, such as cypresses and wisteria, combine with more traditional English cottage garden plants to add pops of colour at different seasons. Ferns, hellebores, spring bulbs, and blossom delight in spring; roses, lavender, clematis, and waterlilies in summer; Japanese maples, herbaceous perennials, and ornamental grasses during the autumn months.

Today, Iford continues to evolve under the stewardship of the Cartwright-Hignett family, while Peto's vision remains undimmed.

FOCUS ON

Harold Peto

Harold Peto (1854–1933) primarily worked as an architect from the late 1870s but gradually became more interested in how buildings interrelated with the landscapes around them. This followed trips to Italy and the Mediterranean, where he admired the design and plantings of the gardens there. When he acquired Iford Manor, he saw the opportunity to experiment with his developing design principles and create a showcase for his work.

The Oudolf Field, with the Radić Pavilion at its head, is a masterclass in perennial meadow planting, featuring many Oudolf favourites, such as echinaceas, heleniums, veronicastrums, rudbeckias, and sedums.

Hauser & Wirth

WHERE *Bruton, Somerset, BA10 0NL* WHEN *Late summer for the full effect of blocks of colour; end of autumn/early winter for seedheads and dried stems* WHAT *A densely planted tapestry of perennials, grasses, and bulbs, selected for their form and longevity*

The garden attached to this international art gallery on the site of a former farm in Somerset has become a magnet for lovers of the perennial meadow style of planting. It was designed by Piet Oudolf, Dutch master of this naturalistic approach.

Although known as the Oudolf "Field", there is nothing agricultural about this garden, which has been carefully designed and planted, and rigorously maintained since it was installed in 2014. Sloping up and away from the gallery and framed on three sides by an existing native hedge, it was planted up in full colour by Dutch landscape designer and plantsman Piet Oudolf, star pioneer of the naturalistic planting movement, which foregrounds textured perennials, biodiversity, and year-round interest.

Oudolf was given free rein to create a garden for Hauser & Wirth that would complement the restored farm buildings and the programme of exhibitions and events that take place here. Drawing on his long experience of using perennials and grasses in blocks and drifts, he filled 17 organic-shaped beds with some 26,000 plants, grown by Orchard Dene Nurseries, which create sweeps of colour and texture that change with the seasons. At the entrance to the garden is an asymmetrical pond, its waters hidden from view in the gallery's colonnade by a ring of marginal plants, including pink-flowering *Butomus umbellatus* and *Iris sibirica* 'Perry's Blue'.

NO FIXED PATH

Visitors have a choice of routes through the garden: along a series of narrow grassy paths that wind through the metal-edged beds on either side of the central gravel path; around the looping perimeter path next to beds filled with taller plants, or a more direct route up the central gravel path. This takes you past sculptural discs of emerald-green grass oversown with clover, to the fibreglass Radić Pavilion, designed by Chilean architect Smiljan Radić, which perches like a giant boulder at the top of the garden.

From here, the view back to the gallery reveals the tapestry effect of the multiple blocks of plants that have been selected for their form,

their longevity, and for being good companions. In some beds, massed plantings of the refined prairie grass *Sporobolus heterolepis*, sprinkled with perennials that add pops of colour such as *Dianthus carthusianorum*, create a meadow-like effect. In others, the soft, feathery grass *Stipa tenuissima* provides rhythm through groups of perennials that stand robustly for many months. These meadow-like beds are framed by taller plants that fill the outer beds, such as *Eutrochium maculatum* Atropurpureum Group, filipendula, and cimicifuga.

SEASONAL CHANGES

This is a garden to visit at different times of the year. In spring, growth in the borders is low and the palette muted, with bursts of colour from tulips, camassias, and alliums (including *Allium nigrum*, *A. atropurpureum*, and *A. cristophii*), which emerge from a matrix of fresh foliage. As the perennials shoot up, a rich mix of burnt orange, purple, pink, white, and plum shades ripple across the borders from Piet Oudolf favourites such as rudbeckias, echinaceas, heleniums, veronicastrums, and sedums. These perennials also provide pollen and nectar for a host of bees, hoverflies, butterflies, and other insects, and the standing stems give shelter during the winter months.

GARDEN INSPIRATION

Stems and Seedheads

A priority for Piet Oudolf when he's selecting plants for this kind of scheme is how each species changes in form and colour through the growing season. He favours species that have interesting and robust stems and seedheads, such as varieties of allium, rudbeckia, veronicastrum, echinacea, and helenium. Visitors to the Oudolf Field can see at first hand the beauty of the standing stems in winter.

Clockwise from top
Helenium *'Moerheim Beauty' recurs in the borders amid sunlit grasses* Molinia caerulea *'Edith Dudszus' and* Sporobolus heterolepis.

The seedheads of Echinacea pallida *stand as dark sentinels through various grasses in winter.*

Jewel-coloured Dianthus carthusianorum *floats above a matrix of grasses.*

The Newt in Somerset

WHERE *Bruton, Somerset, BA7 7NG* WHEN *Year-round interest; spring for apple blossom; summer for Colour Gardens, Cottage Garden, and Victorian Garden*
WHAT *A historic garden that has been redesigned and extended on a huge scale, and with horticultural and architectural expertise, since its current owners bought the estate in 2013*

Set in a vast estate of farmland and woods, the Newt in Somerset, formerly the home of designer Penelope Hobhouse, combines the fun elements of garden-making with the high standards required to successfully grow plants, indoors and outdoors, in all seasons.

Arriving at this 12-hectare (30-acre) garden, it is clear that the Newt has been created with horticultural vision and ambition. Even cars are parked between strips of fragrant herbs and other perennials, and surrounded by an orchard of crab apples that was planted in 2017 and has now been awarded National Collection status.

The entrance boardwalk winds through mixed woodland, where some of the trees are hundreds of years old. Beyond is the egg-shaped, sloping Walled Garden, installed in the eighteenth century by Henry Hobhouse II, and planted with colour-themed borders in the 1980s by Canadian designers Nori and Sandra Pope. Today, it is laid out in a series of concentric beds filled with some 330 cultivars of dessert apple, grouped by county, which have won the Newt its second National Collection.

PLAYFUL INTERACTION

Fanning out from here are the themed gardens, including the Victorian Garden, filled with colourful bedding plants and a vast water tank and cascade where giant newts (the estate is home to all three native species) and frogs spout jets of water, to the delight of children. You will also find the Cottage Garden, the Japanese Garden, and, as a tribute to the Popes, the Colour Gardens, a trio of intimate colour-themed gardens, divided by wattle hurdles. These overlook the grass apron that sweeps down from seventeenth-century Hadspen House, now a boutique hotel, and across to a thicket of cloud-pruned yews, which give this part of the garden instant maturity. The immaculately tended vegetable garden marks the limit of the formal garden here.

There's a choice of remarkable destinations for those who venture further into the estate. A treetop walkway, winding 12 metres (40ft) above ground, leads to an interactive museum that recreates styles of garden-making. Further on is a reimagined Roman villa, built on the site of an original villa excavated in the 1960s, and with a small garden planted with species that would have been growing in Britain at the time.

Another feat of craftsmanship is the Grotto, a cave studded with shells and crystals, and home to red-eyed bats and a scaly wyvern. A return to the other side of the formal gardens offers the gentler experience of observing wild bees at work in their hives from the Beezantium.

Right *Successive pools lead up to the house, inspired by Islamic design.*

Far right *Espalier-trained apple trees adorn the brick wall of the Parabola.*

FOCUS ON

Fruit Training

The interior and exterior of the historic, egg-shaped Walled Garden have been designed by French architect Patrice Taravella as a living example of French techniques of fruit growing. Expertly trained against the walls by the Newt's gardeners in a variety of shapes, including single and double Us, fans, goblets, and the double helix, the 689 apple trees – mainly old British varieties – are not only superbly productive, they make striking outlines in winter.

Bamboos, tree ferns, and bananas relish the streamside moisture, while distinctive red bridges provide an East Asian feel.

Abbotsbury Subtropical Gardens

WHERE *Abbotsbury, Weymouth, Dorset, DT3 4LA* WHEN *Spring, summer, and autumn* WHAT *A sheltered coastal site enjoying a mild climate with a walled garden, lily pools, streamside plantings, and a woodland garden glade featuring Himalayan plants*

Abbotsbury lies just a short wander from Chesil Beach on Dorset's Jurassic Coast. This special place is home to a range of plants from lush palms and bamboos to flowering gingers, towering eucalyptus, and spectacular magnolias and rhododendrons.

This remarkable garden, with its profusion of tender plants, owes its existence to the microclimate provided by the site's coastal location, valley setting, and sheltering hills. The benign conditions have long been appreciated; in the eighteenth century Abbotsbury Castle was built, and land beside it soon became a garden celebrated for its impressive collections of plants. The castle is long gone, although the old stone walls of the former kitchen garden remain and now shelter impressive clumps of bananas, marvellous fern *Woodwardia radicans*, with its arching fronds, and many tender climbers.

The impression that you have been transported to warmer climes is convincing – an aviary of laughing kookaburras only adds to the effect.

The only really formal space is the Victorian Garden, with its neatly trimmed lawns, century-old *Trachycarpus fortunei*, and eye-popping summer bedding schemes. Higher ground to the north is a suntrap. The rocky slope known as the Mediterranean Bank overflows with sun-loving plants, including *Agave*, *Dasylirion*, and *Puya*, as well as clumps of summer-flowering *Agapanthus* and *Watsonia*, while *Erigeron karvinskianus* cascades with little daisy flowers year-round. Further up is a terrace with a pair of recently restored lily ponds dating back to 1889.

VALLEY ESCAPE

The northern part of the site is also home to the Australasian Garden, with huge eucalyptus and mimosa trees, as well as South American planting, including myrtles and *Crinodendron hookerianum*, with its dazzling red lanterns.

Down in the valley, streamside plantings are impressively lush, with towering clumps of bamboo, vast patches of *Gunnera*, and groves of tree ferns underplanted with yellow-flowered *Ligularia*, candelabra primulas, and exotic ginger lilies. Red bridges crossing the stream give an East Asian air. Spring is a key time here; camellias are one of the great specialities, while in the woodland the Sino-Himalayan Glade includes fine magnolias and rhododendrons. Remember to play Indiana Jones on the Burma Rope Bridge and climb to the Viewpoint with its vista of ruined St Catherine's Chapel nearby.

TIMELINE OF EVENTS

1765

Abbotsbury Castle and kitchen gardens built by 1st Countess of Ilchester.

1808

The 3rd Earl begins woodland plantings around the castle.

1853–1905

Plant collections begin to expand under the 4th and 5th earls.

1899

Abbotsbury's plant collection is among the finest in England.

1913

Fire damages the castle.

1934

The castle is demolished; the gardens decline between the wars.

1960s

Restoration of the gardens by Lady Teresa Agnew and Lord Galway begins.

1990

Damage to the gardens after Burn's Day Storm; much replanting follows.

The Stream Field, where water from a rock gully flows down to the lake below. Marginal plants line the water course, with autumnal hues of Liquidambar styraciflua *'Worplesdon'.*

RHS Garden Rosemoor

WHERE *Great Torrington, Devon, EX38 8PH* WHEN *The garden offers year-round interest*
WHAT *A 26-hectare (65-acre) historic garden, renowned for its collection of plants, including rhododendrons, camellias, roses, and champion trees, and its more recently designed garden rooms*

Gifted to the RHS in 1988 by renowned plantswoman Lady Anne Berry (formerly Palmer), Rosemoor is a blend of her original plantings, which include historic rhododendrons and cherry trees, and more recent areas designed to adapt to different conditions.

Sheltered by woodlands, Rosemoor Garden lies in the Torridge Valley and is, unusually for a public garden, bisected by a main road. The re-landscaping of the garden, soon after it was gifted to the RHS, created an inspired way of linking the two parts: an underpass, lined with blocks of mossy stone to give the sense of venturing through an abandoned quarry, now connects the original garden with the more recent Formal Garden, with a lake that doubles as an irrigation reservoir, and a diverted stream with lush marginal planting.

The Formal Garden – a series of themed "rooms" linked by a central walkway edged with long borders that stretch for 150 metres (492ft) – is the first part of the garden to be explored on entering. The roses, which festoon arches, supports, and rope swags, are spread across two of the garden rooms, one filled with shrub roses, including the fragrant *Rosa* 'Rosemoor (Austough[PBR])', the other with modern hybrid tea and floribunda roses. Alongside this is the Cottage Garden, with old-fashioned favourites surrounding a charming wattle-and-daub thatched summerhouse.

Across the central path is a room celebrating foliage plants, and then there is another that is vibrant with shades of red, orange, yellow, and purple. This is known as the Hot Garden, and its opposite, the Cool Garden, was redesigned in 2019 by Jo Thompson, who used plants in pastel shades surrounding a teardrop-shaped

"Every season is full of plant drama and interest. If you like plants, you will feel like a child in a sweet shop."

JONATHAN WEBSTER, CURATOR, RHS ROSEMOOR

pool to create a landscape that elegantly deals with heavy rainfall and flash flooding.

At the southern end of the Formal Garden is Rosemoor's recently redesigned Winter Garden, which is bright even in the darkest months with coloured stems and bark, and new plantings of perennials and grasses.

THE ORIGINAL GARDEN

Through the underpass are many trees and shrubs of the original garden, including Lady Anne's Garden where many of Rosemoor's champion trees (see page 93) can be found, as well as rare rhododendrons that flourish alongside recent additions of dogwoods (*Cornus* is one of Rosemoor's seven National Collections).

In the former walled Kitchen Garden, visiting gardeners can get ideas for plants that create an exotic look while still being hardy, including varieties of canna, ginger lily, banana, and tree fern. Meanwhile, in the Mediterranean Garden raised beds and gritty soil create the best growing conditions – given Devon's wet climate and often cold winters – for a wide range of evocative plants from the world's five Mediterranean climates, including pole-like cypress trees, self-seeding Californian poppies, and *Stipa tenuissima*.

Rosemoor is also a place for year-round strolls through the woodlands that surround the garden and for exploring the areas of wildflower meadow, which the team of gardeners have been establishing as part of a programme to increase biodiversity on the estate.

GARDEN INSPIRATION

Growing Roses

Rosemoor's collection of more than 250 varieties of rose is the largest in the South West. Roses prefer heavy soil but don't thrive when waterlogged. Before planting, Rosemoor's gardeners improved the drainage of the clay soil, laying pipe drains and adding organic matter. They chose disease-resistant varieties such as the pink-striped *Rosa gallica* 'Versicolor' and *Rosa* 'Long John Silver' with its scented white blooms late in the season.

TIMELINE OF EVENTS

1923

Sir Robert Horace Walpole buys the Rosemoor estate.

1931

On his death, Rosemoor becomes home to Lady Anne Berry and her mother.

1940s

The house is used by the Red Cross during the Second World War.

1959

Lady Anne meets plantsman Collingwood Ingram, who introduces her to collecting.

1988

Lady Anne gifts the estate to the RHS.

1989

The garden is re-landscaped by Elizabeth Banks Associates to create a large formal garden with a lake and diverted stream.

Clockwise from top

Repeated blocks of vibrant perennials pull the design together in the Hot Garden.

Foxgloves in Peter Rabbit's garden – a family favourite – in the Vegetable Garden.

Scented Rosa *'Rosemoor (Austough[PBR])' was bred by David Austin in 2004 for the RHS's bicentenary.*

Sumptuous summer herbaceous perennials wrap the historic buildings of the Garden House.

The Garden House

WHERE *Buckland Monachorum, Yelverton, West Devon, PL20 7LQ* WHEN *Year-round interest; January to March for the Snowdrop Festival; summer for herbaceous borders; autumn for colour* WHAT *An extraordinary collection of rare plants alongside familiar varieties, displayed with artistry to create seasonal interest all year*

Like many British gardens made in the latter twentieth century, the Garden House owes its existence, in part, to having formed the grounds of a former vicarage. Few, however, have had such visionaries as Lionel and Katharine Fortescue involved in their creation.

The Fortescues bought the Garden House in 1945 and embarked on an ambitious journey to revive the grounds. Their approach was both innovative and respectful of the site's heritage: their initial masterstroke was to create the 0.8-hectare (2-acre) Walled Garden, built into the ruins of the previous sixteenth-century vicarage, where they established a remarkable collection of plants arranged with both artistic flair and botanical expertise. The space is particularly vibrant in late summer, when dahlias and herbaceous perennials sing.

BOTANICAL EXCELLENCE

Further areas were then developed, while the garden was enriched with rare specimens from nurseries and other keen plantspeople. The couple trialled all manner of species in the climate and acid loam soil provided by the site, while meticulous record-keeping laid the foundation for the garden's development as a valuable botanical collection. Lionel in particular was a stickler for recording plant performance. A hellebore and mahonia bear his name to commemorate his plantsmanship.

The appointment of Keith Wiley as head gardener in 1978 brought fresh creative energy. His naturalistic planting style and innovative approaches to landscape design helped establish the Garden House's reputation as a centre of horticultural excellence. The Long Walk is a key seasonal highlight, taking you from the house, through the Summer Garden, which bursts with grasses and herbaceous perennials, to the Cottage Garden, where soft, romantic planting springs up around the ruins of an old cottage, finally leading to the Wild Flower Meadow, a haven for pollinators. In autumn, the Acer Glade is ablaze with reds and golds, while in late winter the Garden House hosts its famous Snowdrop Festival.

Following Lionel's death in 1981, the garden passed to the Fortescue Garden Trust, marking a new chapter. The garden has now been at the forefront of horticulture for over 50 years, and continues to inspire, educate, and train.

Inspired by wild plants, the Tribute Garden creates a naturalistic look using cultivated species and varieties.

Wildside

WHERE *Buckland Monachorum, Yelverton, West Devon, PL20 7NP* WHEN *Spring for bulbs, trees, and shrubs; summer for herbaceous perennials; autumn for grasses and foliage* WHAT *A multifaceted garden with a diverse range of ornamental woody and herbaceous plants grown in conditions that emulate their natural habitats*

Once a flat, featureless field, the site of Wildside has been transformed into a rich tapestry of garden spaces. It showcases one of the most innovative approaches to garden design in the UK, a testament to the expertise, artistry, and determination of its creators.

The garden at Wildside represents a bold departure from traditional English garden design. Created by Keith and Ros Wiley over little more than 20 years, its naturalistic plantings and innovative use of terrain mirror ecological niches found in the wild. Having spent 25 years refining their craft together at nearby Garden House (see page 122), the couple moved to this then-unprepossessing plot, where their experience of observing plants in their natural habitats was put to expert use.

EMULATING NATURE

The conditions at Wildside have been enhanced to both benefit from the local Devon climate and accommodate its limitations. Raised mounds and excavated gulleys form the overall landscape, within which habitats and plant populations from around the world have been recreated. Carefully selected trees and shrubs in the Lower Garden, including a collection of stunning magnolias, create the canopy in the maturing woodland sections. Their shade helps maintain humidity, and provides a shower of soil-enriching autumn leaves for the understorey of diminutive plants beneath. This area is laced with sinuous paths linking shaded hollows and sunny glades to provide a wealth of planting opportunities.

Meanwhile, on the up-slope by the house, a courtyard incorporating a monumental wisteria-clad arbour is planted with a wealth of species from Mediterranean regions. This leads imperceptibly into what are referred to as the Canyons, where hills and mounds create rock and scree habitats. This large area takes inspiration from a wealth of environments, including the vast open spaces of Namaqualand in Southern Africa, the sun-baked hills of the Mediterranean, and airy birch forests in the Northern Hemisphere. Central to this concept of diversity is the Tribute Garden, inspired by the flora of South Africa and designed by Keith to commemorate Ros, who sadly died in 2019.

This extraordinary garden has plenty to teach any gardener about working with both soil and microclimates, especially in the face of rapid climate change.

The Lost Gardens of Heligan

WHERE *Pentewan, St Austell, Cornwall, PL26 6EN* WHEN *Best from spring until early autumn* WHAT *Restored estate with extensive walled and pleasure gardens, plus, in a steep-sided valley, a "jungle" of bamboos, palms, and tree ferns*

The story of Heligan's decline, rediscovery, and restoration is one of the most romantic in gardening. While today the lush Jungle with its boardwalks and rope bridge is superb, walled productive gardens offer poignant glimpses into the past.

Although today one of Cornwall's most famous gardens, Heligan was, until the mid-1990s, almost completely forgotten, its 81 hectares (200 acres) slumbering below impenetrable brambles after decades of neglect. Rediscovered in 1990, the garden's restoration and a TV series followed, its story resonating strongly with viewers.

RISE, FALL, AND REBIRTH

Heligan was home to the Tremayne family, and much of what we see was set out by John Tremayne between 1851 and 1901, when the monumental rhododendrons, glorious camellias, and exotic tree ferns and Chusan palms were planted, and the Sundial Garden laid out. His son Jack added more before the First World War, including a charming Italian Garden and the Ravine. In 1919 Jack returned from duty to Heligan, but was so saddened by the staff killed during hostilities that he moved to Italy and the estate fell into disarray.

Visiting the flourishing gardens today, this later tale of decline seems scarcely credible. The Jungle is a place of pilgrimage for plant lovers, with exciting, exotic new plantings thriving alongside relics such as original tree ferns, bamboos, and a towering *Podocarpus totara*.

The productive gardens offer glimpses of a now-lost era: in the walled Flower Garden, with its Peach House, Vinery and Banana House, sweet peas and other annual flowers are grown for cutting. The Melon Yard features a Victorian Melon House, a curved wall planted with espalier fruit, and rows of restored cold frames. There is even a pineapple pit for cultivation of what was once the most desirable of fruits.

In the corner of the Melon Yard stands the Thunderbox Room, where names of past gardeners, many killed in the First World War, are written on old plaster – a touching sight. In the quieter moments the atmosphere here is at its most spellbinding, when those whispers from the past are almost audible.

GARDEN INSPIRATION

In the Jungle

Get Heligan's Jungle look with key plants such as palms (e.g. *Trachycarpus fortunei*), bamboo (e.g. *Fargesia rufa*), tree ferns (e.g. *Dicksonia antarctica*), camellias (e.g. *Camellia japonica* 'Lavinia Maggi' or pink *C.* × *williamsii* 'St Ewe'), and scented ginger lilies (e.g. *Hedychium gardnerianum*).

Top *The restored cold frames in the Melon Yard today provide crops for the productive gardens.*

Left *Tree ferns revel in the mild, moist conditions at Heligan.*

Trebah

WHERE *Mawnan Smith, Falmouth, Cornwall, TR11 5JZ* WHEN *Spring, summer, and autumn* WHAT *A magical valley garden running down to the Helford river, filled with rare and tender plants*

Nestling in a sheltered valley on the Cornish coast, this stunning place, first created some 200 years ago, is filled with extraordinary plants that thrive in the warm, wet conditions, from giant bamboos and aged tree ferns to sky-scraping palms.

We owe the survival of this sublime valley garden to Major Tony Hibbert, who in 1981, with his wife, bought the house, planning on a restful retirement, only to learn that they had also taken on a once-important garden. He set about restoring it, and six years later Trebah was ready for visitors – a 10.5-hectare (26-acre) garden where venerable specimens of choice, often tender plants can be enjoyed.

Visitors usually enter from the top of the valley, past the house via the Lawn Path, beside a rock garden with huge agave and soaring, blue-flowered echium. From here you can enjoy views down to the Helford river. In spring, tree-sized rhododendrons flaunt showy flowers, while lofty palms tower above freshly emerging tree-fern fronds. An exciting development is the new Court Garden near the house, made on an old tennis court. It is a peaceful walled space with sensory planting within a formal layout.

STREAMSIDE DELIGHTS

Trebah's style is relaxed and highly informal but above all lush; at times you feel enveloped by the planting. At the top of the valley, surrounded by granite boulders, lies the fern-fringed Koi Pool and its golden fish, and below it the glorious Water Garden, with an avenue of majestic tree ferns underplanted with candelabra primulas, *Hedychium*, and iris. Rhododendron Valley features some towering plants – rhododendrons, of course, but also the UK's tallest palms, *Trachycarpus fortunei*, the loftiest standing at almost 15 metres (50ft).

A stream runs the full course of the valley, filling pools and providing moisture. It passes the Bamboozle – a collection of often-huge bamboos – then, as you make your way down, there are some remarkable specimens: *Davidia involucrata*, the white-bract-adorned flowerheads of its lowest branches in spring dancing above a carpet of bluebells; rare weeping evergreen *Laureliopsis philippiana*, a champion tree, and spectacular *Rhododendron* 'Loderi King George' with huge, fragrant, funnel-shaped blooms.

It's impossible not to mention the colossal expanse of *Gunnera* × *cryptica*, which here reaches monumental proportions in the lost world that is Gunnera Passage – just one of a succession of delights at Trebah.

GARDEN INSPIRATION

Big and Bold

Even if your garden is small, include outsized plants to replicate Trebah's sense of being submerged in plants – tall bamboos such as *Phyllostachys* and *Borinda* will provide height, while bold-leaved *Fatsia*, *Tetrapanax*, and *Magnolia grandiflora* provide drama. Palm *Trachycarpus fortunei* is a must. Water is also important, with numerous stream-fed ponds along the course of the valley to the sea, so try to include a pool of some sort, and if you have a lawn, convert it into a mini-meadow.

Lush, towering planting of palms, rhododendrons, and ferns makes this valley garden truly immersive.

Tremenheere Sculpture Gardens

WHERE *Nr Gulval, Penzance, Cornwall, TR20 8YL* WHEN *Spring, summer, and autumn* WHAT *An informal garden featuring a dynamic collection of contemporary artworks, set against a backdrop of subtropical planting and impressive coastal views*

A Cornish garden created for the twenty-first century, Tremenheere combines exciting, often boundary-pushing planting with inspiring sculptures and installations, many by renowned artists, positioned thoughtfully across the 9-hectare (22-acre) site.

Just a mile east of Penzance lies one of the most stimulating UK gardens of recent years, the vision of plantsman, art enthusiast, and local doctor Neil Armstrong. Tremenheere's transformation into a distinctive, contemplative garden in a short time is testament to Neil's determination and the growing conditions here.

Set in a south-facing valley by the coast, on land once worked by monks from nearby St Michael's Mount, Tremenheere had fallen into disuse in recent years. However, a warm microclimate, fertile soil, and woodland shelter offered great potential. Today, a jaw-dropping range of plants flourish, from collections of palms and delicate tree ferns, to cacti, towering *Agave*, and spectacular *Xanthorrhoea* (grass trees). Plants, however, are only part of the story.

THE ART OF GARDENING

Tremenheere merges garden with art gallery, the trail of 48 sculptures drawing you across the site, via paths that follow the contours of the land. The pieces are varied in style, scale, and material, and are usually discrete from each other. The exotic planting and sculptures blend into the landscape to form Neil's vision of a "naturalistic, Arcadian space".

Along the bottom of the valley runs the Woodland Walk with its meandering stream. Here, in humid shade below magnolias, bamboos, and rhododendrons, are cascading conifer *Dacrydium cupressinum*, bold *Cordyline indivisa* with its broad, lance-shaped leaves, and tree ferns – familiar *Dicksonia antarctica*, but also silver-backed *Cyathea dealbata*.

One unmissable area is the Chelsea Garden, which includes slate platforms taken from Darren Hawkes's 2015 RHS Chelsea Flower Show Garden. They now step down to a shaded pool fringed with tree ferns, bananas, bamboos, and *Gunnera*. This intimate area is one of the garden's "silent spaces", reserved for reflection.

Up the valley sides into the sun, you'll find South African *Restio*, *Puya*, *Butia*, and succulents galore. At the top is James Turrell's must-see *Tewlwolow Kernow* ("Twilight in Cornwall"), a sunken "skyspace" chamber with a domed roof – another place to be alone with your thoughts.

Clockwise from right
A slate platform leads out to a shady pool in the Chelsea Garden.

The garden terraces afford stunning views across Mount's Bay.

Black Mound *by David Nash was created using a chainsaw and blow torch.*

FOCUS ON

Art at Tremenheere

The sculptures at Tremenheere are highly varied. Some, such as Penny Saunders' dynamic *Restless Temple* positioned on a hilltop, are imposing; while others have more subtle appeal; Séamus Moran's *Fallen* hangs serpent-like from a branch. Staging is carefully considered. David Nash's *Black Mound* looks perfectly at home in the Oak Woodland and Richard Woods' cartoon-like *Holiday Home* enjoys a commanding position at the top of the site.

Trengwainton

WHERE *Madron, Penzance, Cornwall, TR20 8RZ* WHEN *Spring, summer, and autumn*
WHAT *A sheltered coastal site in one of the mildest parts of mainland UK, with streamside and walled gardens overflowing with tender plants*

For many plant enthusiasts, Trengwainton is among the most exciting UK gardens. With its history of important plant introductions and a moist, near frost-free climate, many of the plants that flourish here are commonly seen only under glass elsewhere.

Trengwainton has an unusual layout. Unlike many Cornish gardens, it does not sit in a sheltered valley. Instead, its 10 hectares (25 acres) are composed of two main areas: the celebrated walled gardens, and the lush streamside gardens that follow the main drive to the house. The climate this close to the sea, influenced by the North Atlantic Current, is wet and exceptionally mild, even for Cornwall. Frost is so rare that plants are in growth year-round, and many tender species can be enjoyed.

WALLS OF WONDER

The walled gardens are perhaps the highlight, a series of different areas that make the most of Trengwainton's remarkable conditions. The Veitchii Garden is so-named due to a vast *Magnolia × veitchii* 'Peter Veitch' planted in 1936, which dominates the area and produces masses of white flowers each spring. You will also find tender Australasian shrubs here, such as banksia and correa, more often found in greenhouses in the UK. Next comes the Campbellii Garden with its majestic *Magnolia campbellii* dating from 1926 – in February it produces huge, pink, chalice-like blooms. The Middle Walled Garden includes rare tree ferns, such as the incredible *Sphaeropteris medullaris*, with its black trunk and vast fronds, as well as pseudopanax, eucryphia, and heptapleurum.

The Kitchen Garden is rather different. Divided into five, it includes Gardener's Cottage, built into the north-facing wall and said to replicate the dimensions of Noah's Ark, as well as curious raised, sloping beds used for vegetables, which maximize sunlight. Next is the Fuchsia Garden, with its lofty cordylines and collection of fuchsias – most notably a vast, scrambling *F. coccinea* – followed by the Foliage Garden, which includes plants with impressive leaves, such as banana *Musa basjoo*.

There is much to enjoy on the other side of the drive. Passing the Jubilee Garden and its towering, blue-flowered echium, the Tree Fern Glade is superb – most specimens are *Dicksonia antarctica*, but you will also find more tender species, such as *D. fibrosa*, planted with rhododendron. The wooded Stream Garden, with more glorious rhododendrons, provides ample moisture for candelabra primulas and zantedeschias, as well as other bog plants, and remains resplendent throughout summer.

Top *The Tree Fern glade features several species of* Dicksonia.

Bottom *Candelabra primulas help lead the eye along the Stream Garden.*

FOCUS ON

Developing the Gardens

Former Trengwainton owner Sir Edward Bolitho was well connected within the Cornish gardening fraternity, and his contacts helped him develop the gardens. In 1926, George Johnstone of Trewithen in Truro and Lawrence Johnston at Hidcote in Gloucestershire offered him a share in plant hunter Frank Kingdon-Ward's expedition to Assam and Burma, and many seeds (including tender rhododendrons) that were sent back were successfully raised at Trengwainton by head gardener Alfred Creek.

The top terraces afford views over the abbey ruins to the islands beyond.

Tresco Abbey Garden

WHERE *Tresco, Isles of Scilly, TR24 0QQ* WHEN *Year-round interest*
WHAT *A remarkable, near-frost-free garden with an island setting, featuring subtropical plantings formed around the ruins of an old abbey*

To visit Tresco Abbey Garden takes a certain amount of determination: sea or air travel is required to reach the lovely Isles of Scilly. The effort, however, is more than repaid, for in this garden subtropical plants have long flourished in the open air, creating an unforgettable atmosphere for a UK garden.

Top of many a gardener's bucket list is a trip to this extraordinary place, a garden distinct from any on the UK mainland, chiefly due to the frost-free climate, which allows tender plants to grow to maturity, but also thanks to its idyllic island setting. The coastal location does have its downsides – salt-laden gales that scream in from the Atlantic would smash the tender plants were it not for extensive shelterbelts of pine and cypress. Occasional cold and severe storms do cause damage, yet most plants survive, most famously the towering *Phoenix canariensis* palms, which are more than 100 years old.

ISLAND PARADISE

The garden at Tresco Abbey was started during the nineteenth century by Augustus John Smith, Lord Proprietor of the Isles of Scilly, near the ruins of a Benedictine priory founded in AD 964; its remaining low walls and arches can still be seen, today cascading with *Erigeron karvinskianus* and succulent aeoniums. Since then, four generations of the Smith family have developed the gardens, first opening them to the public in 1950.

Referred to as "a perennial Kew without the glass", the site covers 7 hectares (17 acres), much of it on a terraced, south-facing hillside. The upper areas are free-draining and exposed, allowing succulents and South African and Australian plants to thrive, while lower down shade and shelter mean different plants flourish. The entrance is at the garden's lower western corner. After crossing a bridge between clumps of vast bamboo, it's worth first making for the

A huge variegated agave dominates the scene, one of the many iconic specimens that flourish in Tresco's mild climate.

FOCUS ON

Extraordinary Trees

At Tresco, many tender trees thrive outdoors. Palms are characteristic of warm climates; alongside *Phoenix canariensis* (Canary Island date palm) are many others, such as *Rhopalostylis sapida* (nikau palm) from New Zealand, with arresting upright green fronds. Other trees include *Metrosideros excelsa* (pohutukawa), with its red flowers, and *Araucaria heterophylla* (Norfolk Island pine), with tiered branches.

terraced Mediterranean Garden about halfway up the site, with its cooling agave fountain and shell house featuring wonderful wall mosaics. Planted here are silvery olive trees and *Chamaerops* palms, which provide a touch of the Italian Riviera.

VIEW FROM THE TOP

The highest part of the garden is the Top Terrace, which offers views over to St Mary's, the largest of the Scilly Isles; it's also a good vantage point from which to admire the gardens stepping down the terraces below. Up here grow vast *Puya*, South American bromeliads with huge rosettes of spine-armed leaves bearing towering spikes of yellow or green flowers, and taller still, the

5-metre- (16½ft-) high spires of yucca-like *Furcraea parmentieri*. This is also where the garden's exceptional collection of South African proteas can be seen, including *Protea cynaroides* (king protea), with its soft-pink flowers that are 30cm (12in) across.

Descending the impressive Neptune Steps (which are topped by an old ship's figurehead named "Father Neptune") ultimately lead to the Long Walk, but halfway down, the stone stairway crosses Middle Terrace, the main route across the garden to the abbey itself (which is a private house). To the right, the terrace leads on back to the heart of the garden, past banks cascading with all manner of exotic plants and fishponds with tinkling fountains. To the left, it passes the Succulent Cliff, a quarry-like area encrusted with succulents, before leading past the Pebble Garden, its beds set out in the design of a Union Jack flag.

Nearby can be found a fine *Jubaea chilensis* (Chilean wine palm) and walls supporting climbers and shrubs, including *Bomarea* and *Iochroma*. Beside the abbey is the West Rockery, with plantings of *Agave*, *Watsonia*, and shimmering *Leucadendron argenteum* or silver tree, whose metallic leaves look as though they have been crafted by a jeweller.

Conditions at the bottom of the garden are rather different. The Long Walk has a sheltered, humid atmosphere, so here, tree ferns flourish in the lush, leafy shade. The magic never ends. A host of other plant surprises await your discovery at this enchanting, unusual garden.

Left *A flower of king protea with its pink, petal-like bracts.*

Right *Giant panicles of* Echium wildpretii *or tower of jewels.*

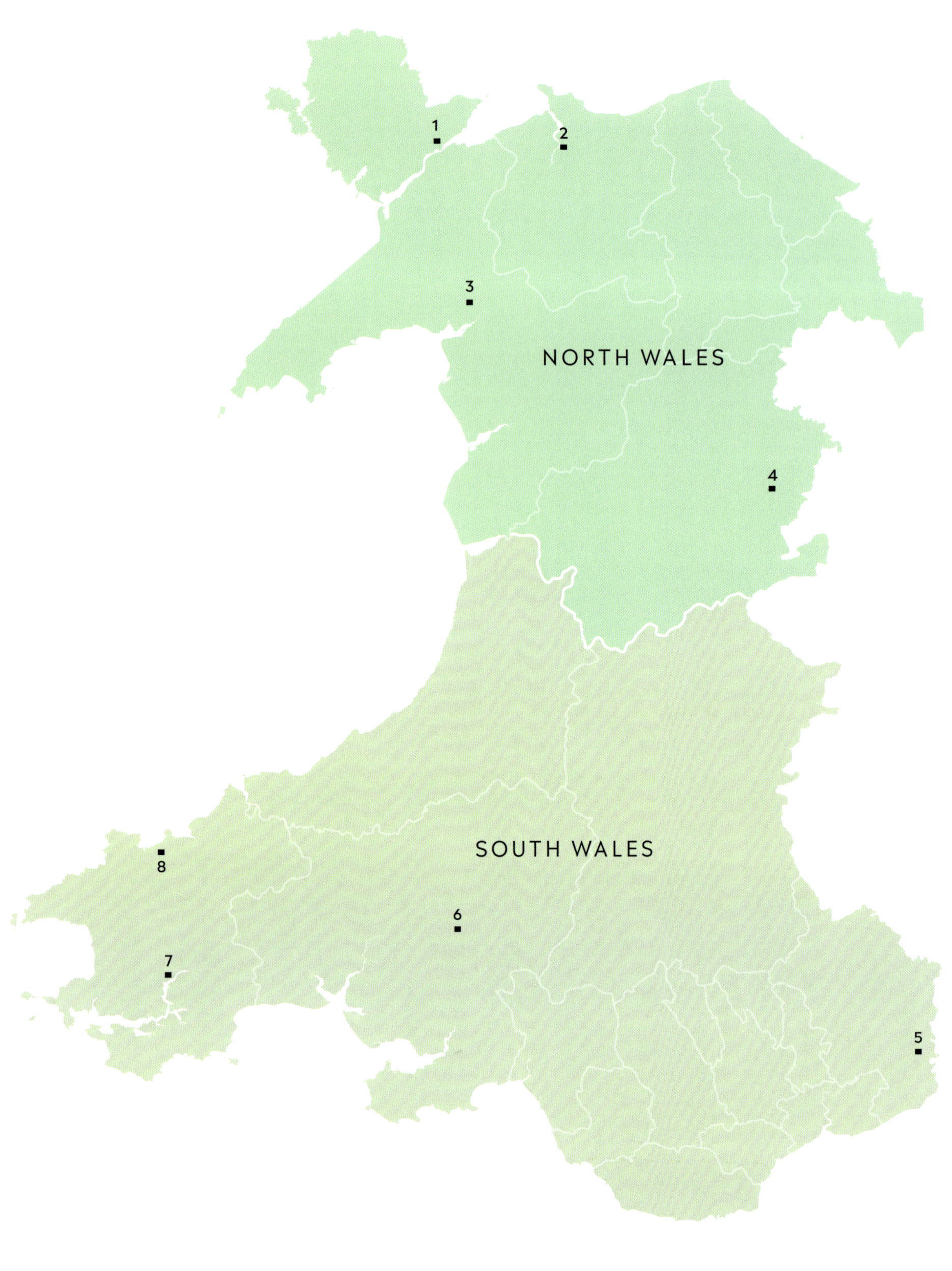
1
2
3
NORTH WALES
4
SOUTH WALES
8
6
7
5

Wales

From the Wye Valley to the mountains of Eryri (Snowdonia), Wales is a country of contrasts. Here you will find gardens of yesterday and gardens of tomorrow. From the 15th-century beginnings of Aberglasney, to the Edwardian Arts and Crafts designs of Plas Brondanw, through to recent masterpieces such as Dyffryn Fernant and Plas Cadnant.

NORTH

1 PLAS CADNANT HIDDEN GARDENS
2 BODNANT GARDEN
3 PLAS BRONDANW
4 POWIS CASTLE GARDEN

SOUTH

5 VEDDW HOUSE GARDEN
6 ABERGLASNEY
7 PICTON CASTLE
8 DYFFRYN FERNANT

Plas Cadnant Hidden Gardens

WHERE *Menai Bridge, Ynys Mon, Anglesey, LL59 5NH* WHEN *April to June for spring displays; June to September for herbaceous borders; September to October for autumn colour* WHAT *A restored Victorian estate situated alongside the coastal waters of the Menai Strait*

Extending to 4 hectares (10 acres), Plas Cadnant's gardens first opened to the public in 2011 after 15 years of painstaking restoration work by owner Anthony Tavernor. The Walled Garden and Fern Dell running down to the River Cadnant are rewards enough.

The origins of the present garden date back to 1804, when John Price, agent to the Marquis of Anglesey, created parkland and gardens around an earlier farmhouse and his recently built "country gentleman's residence". Alongside this new house, a 0.8 hectare (2-acre) walled garden was used to provide fruit, vegetables, and cut flowers. From the late 1940s, however, much of the garden and buildings fell into gentle decline.

In 1996, Staffordshire farmer Anthony Tavernor saw an advertisement for the sale of Plas Cadnant and, given his life-long interest in gardens, history, and architecture, he arranged a viewing. On arrival, he says, "It was a classic case of falling in love with a place on first sight."

Since then Anthony has spent his time not only restoring the buildings and gardens to a high specification rarely seen since the days of the Arts and Crafts movement, but also developing new gardens, vistas, and planting schemes for colour and interest year-round.

DRAMATIC TRANSFORMATION

When Anthony took on Plas Cadnant, the Walled Garden was covered in self-sown sycamore trees, *Rhododendron ponticum*, cherry laurel, and head-high brambles. Today, its manicured lawns are planted with close-clipped yew topiary and fruit trees, bordered by Chilean eucryphias, flowering dogwoods, *Hydrangea serrata* 'Preziosa', and colour-coordinated herbaceous borders. The focal point is an ancient pool, the waters of which, in April and May, reflect drifts of vibrant magenta *Bergenia* 'Overture'.

Below the Walled Garden Anthony has created a magical Valley Garden, planted with hundreds of flowering trees, shrubs, bulbs, and ferns, all of which cascade down the steep slopes to the banks of the River Cadnant. Here, beneath lush canopies, the air is cool and humidity high, making it the ideal environment for moisture-loving woodland plants such as *Rodgersia podophylla* and *Astilbe* 'Color Flash', and groves of tree ferns.

Right *The trunks of established trees in the Valley Garden can be shaggy with moss thanks to the cool humidity.*

Below *Moisture-loving plants such as ferns and rodgersias thrive alongside mounding acers.*

"It was a classic case of falling in love with a place on first sight."

ANTHONY TAVERNOR

The Winter Garden, with its white-stemmed birches, tactile grasses, fragrant witch hazels, and colourful early rhododendrons.

Bodnant Garden

WHERE *Tal-y-Cafn, Conwy, LL28 5RE* WHEN *All year round* WHAT *Expansive garden in Snowdonia, featuring important plant collections spread across 32.3 hectares (80 acres), including monumental Edwardian, Italianate terraces and a sublime wooded valley*

One of the world's finest gardens, everything at Bodnant is done on a grand scale, from the vast plant collections – including many rare and venerable specimens – to the landscaping, with its imposing terraces contrasting with the naturalistic Dell, set in a steep-sided valley.

Sitting within beautiful countryside, Bodnant offers some truly jaw-dropping moments alongside historic plant collections, and features impressive set-pieces, many of them heroic in size and execution. The moist climate and acidic soil favours ericaceous plants, and the garden is known for magnolias, rhododendrons, and camellias, which put on superb displays, mostly in spring, but interest lasts year-round. The Winter Garden dazzles with white-stemmed birches, fragrant witch hazels, and early rhododendrons.

GARDEN OF WONDER

Central is Bodnant Hall, a sprawling mansion atop five mighty terraces that step down the valley towards the River Conwy. To the south lies the Front Lawn with its herbaceous borders and charming Round Garden with fountain and herb plantings. Here, too, is one of Bodnant's most wonderful features, the Laburnum Arch, which peaks in late May as *Laburnum × waterei* 'Vossii' plants, trained over a 55-metre- (180ft-) long pergola, produce thousands of scented flower racemes, forming a tunnel of gold.

The Upper Rose Terrace features a formal layout, and leads to the Croquet Terrace via a wisteria-draped staircase. On the Lily Terrace, the central pond is flanked by cedar trees, with lofty retaining walls supporting climbing and trained plants, such as *Magnolia campbellii* and *Eucryphia*. The elegant curved pergola of the Lower Rose Terrace supports cascading roses and *Wisteria brachybotrys*, and on the final level, the Canal Terrace, immaculate lawns flank a pool, reflecting the handsome Pin Mill.

The steep-sided, wooded valley that shelters the Dell is a magical place. You'll see the River Hiraethlyn winding far below, while towering magnolias and fine conifers soar up to greet you. Rhododendrons form the understorey on the slopes, while at the valley bottom moisture-loving ferns, candelabra primulas, hydrangeas, and astilbes luxuriate. Highlights include the Rockery, and a bridge that crosses a waterfall.

Despite recent storm damage, Bodnant's greatness endures. Relatively new areas include the Far End with its Skating Lake, and the Deep Bath, a restored sunken garden with a former bathing pool now lushly planted with exotics.

Plas Brondanw

WHERE *Llanfrothen, Garreg, Penrhyndeudraeth* WHEN *Year-round for garden structure, interesting statuary, and outstanding views* WHAT *An architectural formal garden, whose vistas borrow the contrasting surrounding landscape of sea, sky, and mountain*

Bertram Williams-Ellis, more often known by his middle name Clough, was a Welsh architect and co-founder of the Council for the Preservation of Rural Wales. Through best known for Portmeirion, the town he created nearby, his garden at Plas Brondanw was closest to his heart.

When Clough Williams-Ellis inherited the property at Plas Brondanw from his father in 1908 the house was crumbling and the garden had become allotments. Over the next 70 years, Williams-Ellis transformed the grounds into an Italian Renaissance-style garden with rooms and fountains. Although the garden is not plant-focused, it does contain hydrangeas, rhododendrons, azaleas, a fabulous 200-year-old *Quercus ilex*, and a fine *Crinodendron hookerianum* – the Chilean lantern tree.

BORROWED LANDSCAPES

The geometry of the garden is dictated by the surrounding landscape. Long vistas terminating in focal points frame various views of the Eryri National Park. There are breathtaking views of Cnicht (the "Welsh Matterhorn"), the great bulk of Moel-ddu, and one of the finest views of Yr Wyddfa (Snowdon) – particularly when capped with snow. It is an outstanding example of how to "borrow" the surrounding landscape.

Steps and terraces constructed of slate from a local quarry also link the garden to the landscape, while tall yew hedging creates narrow passages ensuring surprises round every corner.

WITTY DETAILS

"Eyecatchers" that draw visitors around the garden display Williams-Ellis's style and sense of humour. Yew topiary is clipped into weird and wonderful shapes. Turquoise and mustard metalwork adds year-round illumination to the garden's grey-slate and evergreen bones. Williams-Ellis often bought artefacts for the garden from country-house sales, such as the trio of classical busts, and the fountain spouting from the hose of a baby-faced fireman. A bust of Caesar on a classical pillar with a plaque claiming it came from Napoleon's estate is a piece of three-in-one historical fiction.

Williams-Ellis served in the Royal Welch Fusiliers, and when he married in 1915 he was offered a traditional silver serving plate as a wedding gift. He declined, asking instead for help to build his folly, Pen Tŵr, a ruined castle on a nearby hillside – the final piece he needed to complete his fantasy garden.

Fans of *Doctor Who* may like to know that Plas Brondanw provided filming locations for the 20th-anniversary special *The Five Doctors*, hosting the Time Lord's first and fifth incarnations. The folly stood in for the Eye of Orion, "for some the most tranquil place in the universe".

Above *The domed topiary wittily echoes the Eryri range of mountains that surround the gardens.*

Right *A cherubic fireman stands to attention on his plinth in the lily pond.*

"We just grow what seems most eager to oblige, with the least trouble to ourselves."

CLOUGH WILLIAMS-ELLIS

Box-edged borders brimming with colourful perennials mark out the Orangery Terrace.

Powis Castle Garden

WHERE *Welshpool, Powis, SY21 8RF* WHEN *Peak displays in summer and autumn*
WHAT *A celebrated garden on a south-facing slope set below the ramparts of a castle, featuring Baroque terraces cascading with romantic and, at times, exotic planting*

A spectacular garden, Powis features ornate Italianate terraces that step down from the castle above, adorned with elegant statuary and dazzling container displays. This is a site brimming with unusual and often tender plants that revel in the favourable microclimates found here.

Few gardens provide the dramatic visual impact of Powis Castle. Largely arranged across a terraced hillside below the imposing red castle, the 10.5 hectares (26 acres) include features from different historical periods. The terraces date from the seventeenth century when the Baroque style was in fashion. With their ornate balustrades and classical statuary, they feel as if they've been lifted from an Italian palazzo. Later, a formal water garden filled what is now the Great Lawn.

The garden owes its romantic Edwardian feel today in large part to Violet Herbert, Countess of Powis, whose desire was to transform the garden into "one of the most beautiful, if not the most beautiful in England and Wales". Many would happily argue that, in restoring and replanting the terraces, she succeeded.

STEPPING DOWN THE TERRACES

Originally laid out in 1688, five terraces remain today. Top-most is the High Terrace, a narrow but vertiginous lawned platform to the north-east of the castle, not accessible to the public. The Top Terrace is the level visitors experience first. Sheltering walls form a backdrop to box-hedged borders. These slope so that planting at the back appears higher; in summer they overflow with exotics, from paddle-leaved *Ensete* and *Musa*, to palms, vast *Tetrapanax*, fiery cannas and dahlias, agapanthus, and salvias. In the other direction the full effect of the tiered garden and the Welsh landscape beyond can be appreciated.

Another highlight are the yews – individual "tumps" that give this confection of a garden charismatic structure – and, at the eastern end,

Clockwise from top left

Carefully placed containers of cascading plants soften the terrace balustrades.

The 14-metre (46ft) cloud-pruned yew hedge is one of the garden's most charismatic features.

The view down the castle's terraces towards the enclosed Formal Garden.

the celebrated cloud-pruned hedge, which is trimmed using a cherry picker. Elegant staircases allow you to descend in a stately fashion to the Aviary Terrace, its shady arches sheltering some remarkable tender plants, including fern *Woodwardia radicans*, then down to the broader Orangery Terrace, with its paired borders of perennials and the handsome central Orangery, the façade of which cascades in spring and summer with roses.

At ground level, there are gardens created by Violet, Countess of Powis, after 1912, on the site of what used to be the castle's kitchen garden: the Formal Garden, with its venerable pyramid-trained fruit trees; the Croquet Lawn, featuring rose- and hollyhock-filled borders, and the Fountain Garden, with its central pool. In spring the Daffodil Paddock is resplendent as it turns to gold, while later a succession of wildflowers spangle the meadow.

GARDEN INSPIRATION

Baroque Grandeur

The contrast of bold foliage and vivid flowers set against classical architecture is part of the allure of Powis. Position statuary, salvaged architectural features, and clipped yew alongside the bold forms of *Tetrapanax*, *Canna*, or *Ricinus*, adding colour from dahlias, exotic hedychium, and rudbeckia. Pot displays are extravagant, so elevate containers on pedestals or tables and fill with cascading *Fuchsia*, nasturtium, *Coleus*, and *Lobelia*. Don't hold back – the effect should be sumptuous.

TIMELINE OF EVENTS

1200s

The castle is constructed.

1688

Terraces are first made by architect William Windle.

1703

The Water Garden is made in the fashionable Dutch style but removed by 1809.

1720s

Specimen yews are planted.

1780s

Terraces fall into disrepair.

1800

The gardens undergo restoration.

1891–1929

Formal Garden replaces kitchen garden, with plantings made by Violet, Countess of Powis.

1952

Powis Castle is acquired by the National Trust.

1970

Garden is refined by NT gardens advisor and plantsman Graham Stewart Thomas.

Veddw House Garden

WHERE *The Fedw, Devauden, Monmouthshire, NP16 6PH* WHEN *From June to September* WHAT *A gem of a private garden set within the jewel that is the Wye Valley*

Set in a natural amphitheatre, surrounded by hills rising above Tintern Abbey, Veddw has attracted many admirers over the years. This influential garden was created, over almost four decades, by garden writer Anne Wareham and photographer Charles Hawes.

When Anne and Charles moved to Veddw in 1987, much of the land was ancient grassland. This past still resonates in the garden, both through Anne's large parterre of grasses set within hedges that echo the layout of a local tithe map from 1841, and in the wildflower meadow situated below the house.

The unusual name Veddw may derive from the Welsh word *bedw*, meaning "birch", and there are plenty of birch trees to be found both in the Wye Valley and within the garden. Perhaps that's why this garden has such a sense of belonging; it sits comfortably within the landscape and belies the fact that, in terms of British garden history, it's still very much a juvenile.

PLAYFUL HEDGING

In all there are 0.8 hectares (2 acres) of ornamental garden and the same again of woodland. From the garden entrance at the top of the slope, first impressions are of a series of hedged enclosures, which initially appear maze-like in their design, evoking an almost child-like excitement to explore and discover.

These hedges, although close-clipped and formal, are playful in their asymmetrical design or two-tone colouring – there are several back-to-back green and purple beech hedges. All are used to create a series of garden rooms, each with its own theme, and its own seat, so visitors can study the variety of unusual plants.

The hedges also provide a foil for thoughtful planting schemes of roses, summer flowers, hostas, irises, *Miscanthus giganteus*, and large-leaved bergenias and rheums, all interspersed with a smattering of weeds, intentionally left, in another nod towards Veddw's agricultural past.

GARDEN ROMANCE

The lower garden in front of the house has a softer, romantic feel. There are fewer enclosures, the flowers relax and recline over pathways, and colour, texture, and fragrance abound. Scented roses clamber over pergolas draped with purple-leaved vines, beneath which ornamental shrubs, including blue hydrangeas and pink-flowering *Clerodendrum bungei*, mix freely with a plethora of herbaceous plantings. A small orchard of fruit trees, including varieties long grown on the Welsh/English border, leads to the wildflower meadow, and this in turn leads to the wider wooded landscape beyond.

"A satisfying blend of formality and informality and of wildness and control."

STEPHEN ANDERTON, *THE TIMES*

Above *The erstwhile veg plot is now home to cardoons and purple fennel grown for their ornamental value.*

Left *Wave-clipped hedges lead maze-like to a calm space for contemplation by the Reflecting Pool.*

Aberglasney

WHERE *Llangathen, Carmarthenshire, SA32 8QH* WHEN *All year round; particularly colourful in late spring and early summer* WHAT *One of Wales's most exciting garden restorations of the past 30 years*

Opened in 1999, this Grade II-listed 4-hectare (10-acre) historical garden is one of the finest in Wales. At its heart lies the fully restored Elizabethan Cloister Garden, which is the only surviving example of its kind in the UK today.

The first documentation of a garden at Aberglasney dates from the fifteenth century. However, what makes Aberglasney truly unique is the astonishing survival of so much of the infrastructure from Bishop Anthony Rudd's Garden, which dates from around 1600. It was Rudd who almost certainly built the original Cloister Garden, with its elevated, broad parapet walkway – most of which survives to this day.

From here, visitors get the best views of the surrounding gardens, including a remarkable collection of new and developing spaces. In the Upper Walled Garden, which has been designed by Penelope Hobhouse, classic evergreens such as fastigiate yews have been used to trace the outline of a Celtic cross. Within this framework is a collection of ornamental bulbs, perennials, shrubs, and climbers, all placed in relaxed fashion to delight the eye from April until October, while also appealing to those looking for something unusual, such as the beautiful crape myrtle *Lagerstroemia indica* 'Rosea', which grows against the south-facing wall.

In contrast, the Kitchen Garden retains its past purpose as a productive space. Today, in summer, the beds resemble an artist's palette, with bright splashes of colour from lines of annuals interspersed with vegetables, ranging from glaucous-blue cabbages to red-stemmed Swiss chard, all surrounded by a framework of fragrant sweet peas.

TRANQUIL WATERS

Beyond the formality of the walled gardens lies the Pool Garden, where the crystal-clear water of the Jacobean-designed "mirror" reflects the colourful plantings on the raised beds of the north wall. The water theme continues with the Sunken Garden, a relatively new feature with a tranquil water sculpture by William Pye at its centre – the perfect place for quiet reflection.

In recent years, Aberglasney gardeners have also developed the surrounding woodland into the magical Jubilee Wood. Particularly effective here are the large-leaved foliage plants such as *Gunnera manicata*, which, in late spring, provide dappled shade for blue Himalayan poppies, white astilbes, and purple-red *Primula vialii*.

FOCUS ON

The Ninfarium

Within the ruinous central courtyard of Aberglasney's mansion is the Ninfarium (pictured above), an award-winning garden created beneath a glass atrium, which was inspired by the Gardens of Ninfa in Italy. Housed within this warm, humid, subtropical environment is a wonderful collection of exotic plants from around the world, including tree ferns and rare tender orchids.

Alliums, 'Ravenswing' cow parsley, and 'Perry's Blue' Siberian iris bring a range of purple notes to the Upper Walled Garden.

Picton Castle

WHERE *Haverfordwest, Pembrokeshire, SA62 4AS* WHEN *Year-round interest, with peak flowering in spring* WHAT *A thirteenth-century castle surrounded by beautiful grounds and gardens, including an eighteenth-century Walled Garden and Victorian Woodland Garden*

Located within the Pembrokeshire National Park, close to the beautiful Cleddau Estuary, Picton Castle was originally built at the end of the thirteenth century by Sir John Wogan, and is still inhabited by his descendants. The site benefits from a mild maritime climate, which is ideal for growing a wide range of exotic plants.

Surrounding Picton Castle are 16 hectares (40 acres) of grounds containing the largest collection of cultivated plants in West Wales. However, Picton is perhaps best known for its collection of spring-flowering shrubs, which includes several rare specimens of rhododendron, such as the world's largest, *Rhododendron* 'Old Port', which was originally raised as a hybrid of *R. catawbiense* before 1865. With rich plum-purple flowers speckled with crimson-black markings, it is considered one of the most attractive rhododendrons in cultivation. Varieties originally bred at Picton include *R.* 'Salmon Jubilee' and *R.* 'Picton Maid'.

The garden also holds two National Plant Collections of ferns: *Woodwardia* and *Onoclea*. Less hardy species are displayed in the Fernery (a modern recreation of the Victorian original), while others grow outside in the new Fern Garden.

WITHIN THE WALLS

In summer, it is the large herbaceous borders of the Grade II-listed Walled Garden that command attention. The mixed planting includes annuals that are changed yearly, and recently, head gardener Roddy Milne has introduced a great collection of hydrangeas, cannas, and grasses to the garden. These help to extend flowering well into autumn and provide wonderful reflections in the rectangular lily pond, with its original early-nineteenth-century fountain.

The space has recently been restored, including the red-brick walls, iron entrance gates, original Gardener's Bothy, fruit store, heritage greenhouse, and a rare example of an eighteenth-century grape store. As the garden is a haven for wildlife, a bat house was also built for any bats disturbed during the renovations.

DRAMA AND GRANDEUR

Another relatively recent addition is the Jungle. Here, amid giant banana leaves, Chinese rice-paper plants, and Chusan palms, are tender species of Central American salvias and the eye-catching South American devil's tobacco (*Lobelia tupa*) – all of which give an indication of just how mild the climate is here.

West of the castle the drama continues: a series of woodland walks are bordered by a collection of towering trees, including giant redwoods, an impressive western red cedar, and an awe-inspiring Japanese cedar.

Clockwise from right
Water lilies flowering in the Walled Garden pond.

Huge rhododendron bushes compete with the castle keep for attention.

Richly coloured flowers of Rhododendron 'Old Port' appear in early summer.

FOCUS ON

Rhododendrons

Originating from Asia, North America, and Central to Eastern Europe, the first rhododendron grown in Britain is reputed to have been *Rhododendron hirsutum*, a dwarf, pink-flowering species introduced from the European Alps in 1656. Contrary to popular belief, not all rhododendrons are invasive. In fact, only one species, *R. ponticum*, has invaded parts of the UK countryside, especially in western England and Wales. The rest are content to remain within the boundary of the garden they were planted in.

The silver obelisk rises from a riot of vegetation in the Bog Garden, with Christina's pink cottage glimpsed behind.

Dyffryn Fernant

WHERE *Llanychaer, Fishguard, Dyfed, SA65 9SP* WHEN *From Easter until October; especially colourful in spring and early summer* WHAT *A new garden designed and created by Christina Shand on a 2.4-hectare (6-acre) patch of Pembrokeshire wilderness*

Dyffryn Fernant will soon be on every garden lover's radar, for when a garden is this good word gets around. Its owner has cleverly allowed the garden to evolve within the topography of an old farm and its surrounding wild landscape.

When Christina Shand first arrived at Dyffryn Fernant in 1996 she described the place as being "the runt of land left over from a once-prosperous, self-contained, productive place" – not so promising for someone intent on creating a garden. Undaunted, Christina forged ahead, but she did not bring in lorry-loads of topsoil and take out lorry-loads of rock, nor did she drag a plough through the clay, or drain the marsh. She simply took these "problems" and turned them into positives.

IN HARMONY

By working with the local, natural characteristics of the landscape, Christina has created a garden that has a real sense of place and is at one with its surroundings, a garden that has arisen out of one particular, unique spot and does not impose itself on the landscape but grows from it.

Where there is rock, Christina has created tumps and viewing mounds, such as in the Magic Garden, which has sublime vistas over the garden to hedgerows and pasture dotted with sheep, then beyond to the hazy blue Preseli uplands. Where there is marsh, there is the Bog Garden, full of primeval plants and ferns surrounding a shiny stainless-steel obelisk, and where the soil is shallow there is Nicky's Field, planted for Christina's brother Nicholas, with geometric displays of ornamental grasses that wind-whisper voices from the past.

A NATURAL HOME

At the centre of the garden lies Christina's traditional, gloriously bright Welsh cottage, with a front garden overflowing with containers displaying bursts of colour, from scarlet dahlias to yellow-flowering aeoniums. Pride of place is a large "copper" filled with water that slides round its curvaceous shape, in constant motion but with a still, mirror-glass surface.

Busy the front garden certainly is, but that's the point. As you move further from the house, the rhythm slows, the colours become more muted, the planting more relaxed, until the garden gradually merges into the wilderness beyond. Brilliantly conceived and beautifully executed, this magical garden works as a whole, despite having many distinct areas. Once visited, it will never be forgotten.

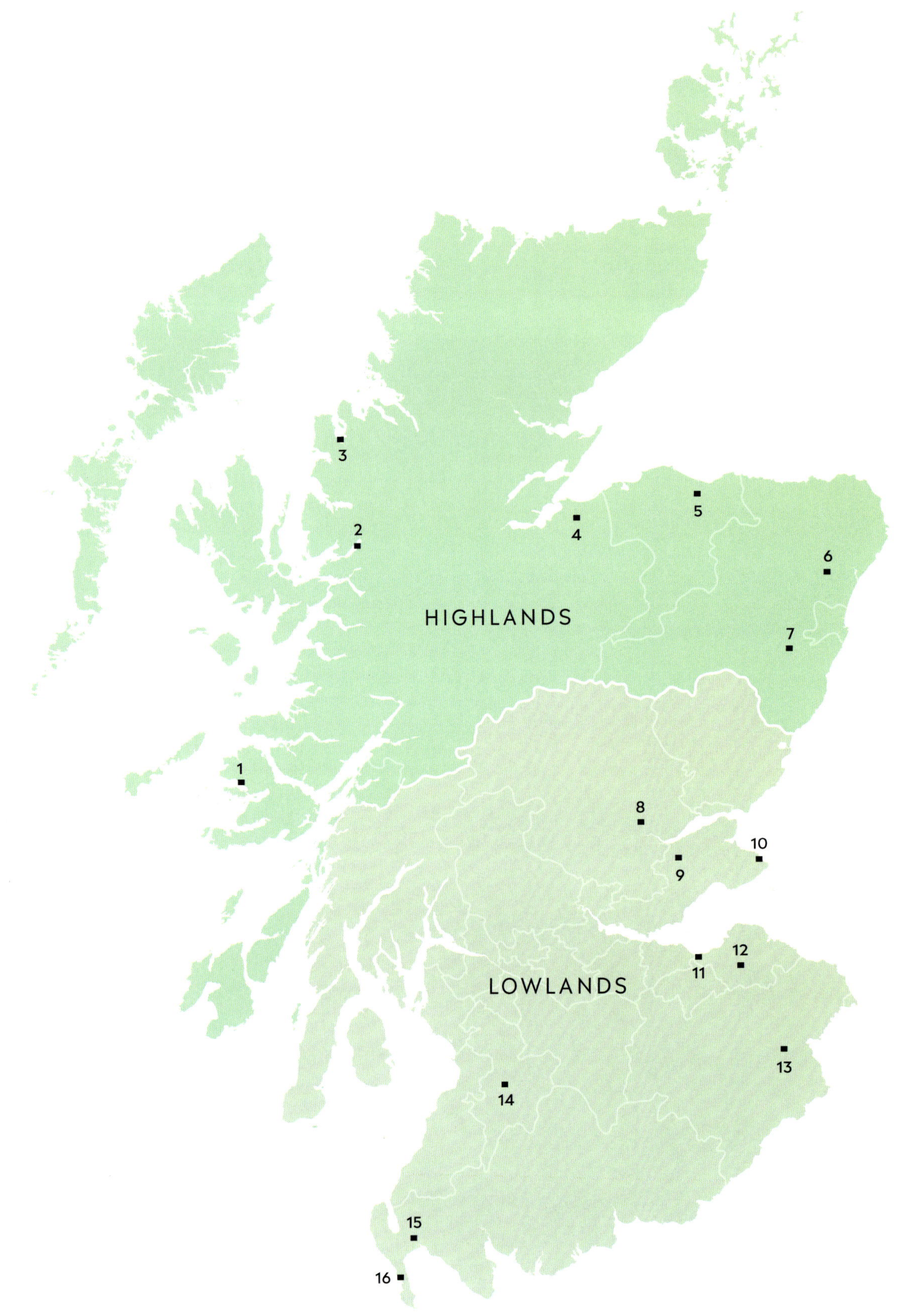
3
2
4
5
6
HIGHLANDS
7
1
8
10
9
12
11
LOWLANDS
13
14
15
16

Scotland

From the subtropical gardens on its rugged west coast, to historic Highland castle gardens, remote islands plots, rose-festooned walled gardens, and contemporary East Lothian and Borders jewels, Scotland offers an eclectic range of lesser known showstopping gardens.

HIGHLANDS

1 LIP NA CLOICHE
2 ATTADALE GARDENS
3 INVEREWE
4 CAWDOR CASTLE
5 GORDON CASTLE WALLED GARDEN
6 PITMEDDEN GARDEN
7 CRATHES CASTLE GARDEN

LOWLANDS

8 SCONE PALACE
9 BACKHOUSE ROSSIE ESTATE
10 CAMBO
11 SHEPHERD HOUSE GARDEN
12 BROADWOODSIDE
13 FLOORS CASTLE
14 DUMFRIES HOUSE
15 GLENWHAN GARDENS
16 LOGAN BOTANIC GARDEN

Lip na Cloiche

WHERE *Ulva Ferry, Isle of Mull, PA73 6LU* WHEN *Year round – the mild coastal conditions support a wide variety of tender plants* WHAT *An imaginative, colour-filled garden carved out of a bracken- and gorse-covered hillside*

Lip na Cloiche, meaning "edge of the rock" in Gaelic, is the jewel of a garden that Lucy Mackenzie has spent the past 20 years creating, with a vibrant collection of flowering shrubs and brightly coloured perennials punctuated with quirky beach finds.

Returning to her native Mull after many years spent in Italy and England, Lucy Mackenzie bought the then-derelict bothy for its spectacular view across Loch Tuath to the Isle of Ulva. There was, after all, little else to recommend the steep 0.4-hectare (1-acre) plot.

Despite the salt-laden Atlantic gales that batter the site, Lucy was determined to retain the vista, so she embarked on a quest to source medium-height and low-growing plants that would withstand the conditions.

A PERSONAL PROJECT

Lucy spent eight years clearing the plot. Laying out the network of paths gave free rein to her artistic talent: the central path is a clever mosaic of random cobbles and reclaimed bricks inset with coils of salvaged rope. The simple bridges over the burn were transformed by driftwood handrails. The burn is edged with glorious swathes of pink and yellow candelabra primulas alongside *Astilboides tabularis* and other moisture-loving plants chosen for their bold, tropical-looking foliage.

HIGH DRAMA

Further up the hill the display of wind-hardy shrubs includes pink and white cistuses and *Buddleja loricata* with its creamy flowers – both tolerate the rocky soil. New Zealand natives work well here: pittosporums, ozothamnus, and olearias proved reliable players: *Olearia arborescens* is Lucy's favourite.

The steep climb, past deep-pink *Chelone obliqua* and *Hydrangea arborescens* 'Annabelle' spilling over the edge of a large raised bed, is rewarded by the view to the Treshnish Isles. A seating area is fronted by a low hedge of *Callistemon rigidus*, the scarlet bottlebrush, which is tolerant of the exposed position. The path winding down the east side of the garden takes in the tall, dramatic *Echium pininana*, which thrives in the mild climate.

Beyond the cottage is a wildflower meadow and woodland with a seating area to enjoy the view. At the entrance is the nursery area, stocked with home-propagated plants. There is no admission charge to this idyllic domestic garden, only an honesty box for welcome donations.

Right *The vibrant but wind-hardy garden looks out over a wildflower meadow and Loch Tuath beyond.*

Far right *Lucy's salvaged treasures are used creatively throughout the garden.*

> "I wanted to rescue what I consider to be part of our heritage."
>
> LUCY MACKENZIE

GARDEN INSPIRATION

Salvaging

Lucy spends time in the winter beachcombing or salvaging material – with the owners' permission – from farm tips and derelict buildings. Finds include iron bedsteads, wheels, and forks, which she uses in fencing, gates, or to edge flowerbeds. A clematis and sweetpea trellis is made of ancient iron cartwheel rims and an iron gate rescued from a local graveyard.

Glorious in spring and summer, Attadale takes on a new dimension with the reds, yellows, and golds of autumn.

Attadale Gardens

WHERE *Strathcarron, Wester Ross, IV54 8YX* WHEN *Spring and summer for the water garden and autumn for the trees* WHAT *An 8-hectare (20-acre) garden perfectly suited to its Highland landscape*

Sited in a rocky landscape with views over Loch Carron, Attadale's gardens were born of destruction. In the 1980s, then-custodian Nicky Macpherson saw an opportunity when two violent storms wreaked havoc on the hillside.

When storm damage uprooted shrubs and brought down trees at Attadale, tossing them across the burn along the drive, Nicky Macpherson saw an opportunity to turn disaster into something unique and wonderful. She sought the help of Fife-based garden designer Michael Innes, who suggested that the fallen trees be left in place to create a trio of ponds along the drive. Arching Monet-style bridges and ribbons of pink primula, purple iris, astilbe, and agapanthus reflecting in the peaty ponds create "a Giverny moment", as the current custodian – Nicky's daughter Joanna – describes it.

PAINTERLY HUES

Colour is key in the planting along the Old Rhododendron Walk, where naturalistic drifts of meconopsis, azaleas, and species trees cover the slope in an intricate tapestry, while the views beyond are spectacular. On a clear day it is possible to see as far as the Cullin Hills on Skye.

South of the house, summer is highlighted in the eighteenth-century Sunken Garden. Centred around a stone sundial and enclosed by drystone walls, the former rose garden provides a succession of colour, with deep-red sedums, blue geraniums, pink astrantias, and clouds of Japanese anemones, chosen to blend with the Highland landscape. On the other side of the front lawn, behind the ancient laburnum tree, a cutting garden is bright with annuals and dahlias.

WOODLAND SURPRISES

Past the elegant kitchen garden, with its geometrically planted beds edged with *Ilex crenata* and punctuated with slender, Italian-inspired yew columns, step-over apple cordons, and rose-strewn arches, comes the Woodland Garden. Here, a succession of surprises

"My mother could always see the potential and always had good ideas. It was effectively a blank canvas."

JOANNA MACPHERSON

unfolds. First is the Rhododendron Dell, where pink, red, and white flower-laden branches arch high overhead. Next comes the shady, sheltered Fernery, with its geodesic dome. Described by Joanna as "a mini-Eden Project", it houses tender ferns, which flourish in the moisture provided by its own small burn. Working with the existing terrain, Nicky transformed an original nineteenth-century field drain into a sunken garden featuring tree ferns such as *Dicksonia antarctica*. Adults and children will enjoy discovering the sculptures, including Hamish Mackie's cheetah, Bridget McCrum's birds, and Joe Smith's slate constructions, all nestled among the foliage.

The path then loops around to the Japanese Garden, which was inspired by a solitary Scots pine clinging to a rocky outcrop. Despite being judged "inappropriate in this setting" by the late Christopher Lloyd of Great Dixter (see page 84), this site, with its acers, cloud-pruned conifers, bamboo, rocks, and carefully raked gravel, exudes a sense of peace that resonates throughout Attadale.

FOCUS ON

Red Squirrels

Joanna's recent collaboration with rewilding charity Trees for Life ensures that the enchanting red squirrel thrives and multiplies at Attadale. The charity assessed the garden's suitability as a habitat, then four males and four females arrived in boxes, which were installed in trees. A feeding programme was introduced and now the squirrels are flourishing.

Clockwise from top

Specialist ferns are housed in a geodesic dome with a mini-waterfall.

The eighteenth-century Sunken Garden, the oldest part of the garden, sits near the house.

Red squirrels are being reintroduced by Joanna Macpherson and thrive in their new habitat.

TIMELINE OF EVENTS

1755

Attadale House is built for Donald Matheson.

1880

The house is rented by the Schroder family.

1910

The estate is bought by the Schroder family, who lay the foundations for the garden, plant trees, and start the collection of rhododendrons, which now numbers over 100.

1952

Bought by Ian Macpherson, whose family originated from Sleat on Skye.

1980

Ian's son Ewan and his artist wife, Nicolette, develop the garden.

2018

Their daughter Joanna Macpherson, and her late husband, Alec Cormack, take over the garden.

Clockwise from top *A view from the gardens of Loch Ewe and Beinn Airigh Charr.*

Pink nerines catch the eye, planted at the top of the Walled Garden.

Petals strew the path beneath a rhododendron in spring.

Inverewe

WHERE *Poolewe, Achnasheen, IV22 2LF* WHEN *Year round, but spring is best for the famous rhododendron collection* WHAT *A lochside garden created from a rocky wilderness with a wide variety of plants and wildlife*

Punctuated by coves, inlets, and wild, sandy beaches, the barren, gale-blasted coastal road to Inverewe gives no hint of the large garden that sits on a peninsula between two lochs with a rocky hill behind – least of all one that is home to exotic and tender plants.

The best view of the garden at Inverewe is on a boat trip from the loch. "You see the shelterbelt, without which the garden wouldn't exist, and how the garden sits in the landscape," explains head gardener Kevin Ball.

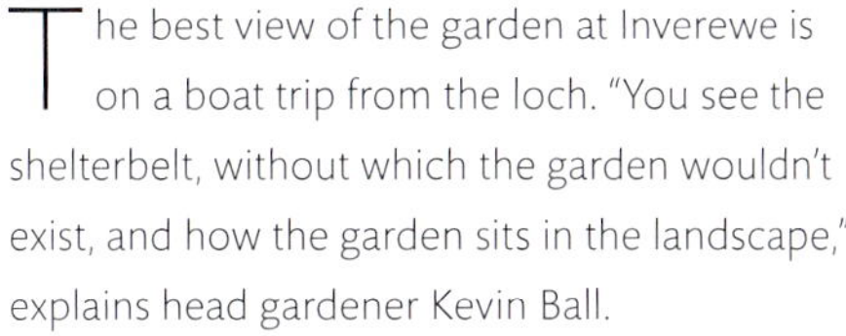

The National Trust for Scotland's flagship garden stands in a class of its own. Established a good 15 years before the railway reached Achnasheen in 1877, by passionate plantsman Osgood Mackenzie, Inverewe is remarkable for the scale of its vision and the beauty of its plants, many from the Southern Hemisphere. It boasts a spectacular collection of trees, including giant redwoods, firs, hemlock, Scots pines, and the Southern beech *Nothofagus betuloides*, and is renowned for its collection of over 200 different rhododendrons. Equally striking are the loch views as you explore the winding network of garden paths.

AN UNLIKELY GARDEN

The garden radiates from Inverewe House, the mansion built by Mackenzie's widowed mother, with spectacular views over Loch Ewe and Beinn Airigh Charr. Early plants arrived by boat along with the topsoil needed to establish them. Unfazed by the terrain, Mackenzie laid out a walled vegetable and flower garden set against a retaining wall in the curve of the beach.

Gifted to the Trust in 1952 by Mackenzie's daughter Mairi Sawyer (also a talented gardener), the garden continues to flourish. The mild climate ensures year-round interest, including many plants once thought impossible to grow this far north. In winter the sunlight filters atmospherically through the trees, illuminating drifts of snowdrops. In spring rhododendrons and azaleas, primulas, and meconopsis are the main attraction. The magnificent collection of erythroniums has prompted the introduction of an annual Erythronium Festival.

As well as vegetables, summer brings an explosion of colour to the Walled Garden, with drifts of orange and yellow crocosmia, bright-blue agapanthus, and jade-green galtonia. In sympathy with the original vision, the garden is not allowed to stand still, though Kevin ensures that "any changes are connected to history".

Cawdor Castle

WHERE *Cawdor, Nairn, IV12 5RD* WHEN *From the end of April to the beginning of October* WHAT *A trio of gardens cultivated on biodynamic principles and celebrating generations of family input*

A visit to Cawdor Castle and its gardens represents something of a double act. The medieval castle in its magnificent ancient landscape gives way to three different gardens where the traditional blends seamlessly with contemporary planting and symbolic sculpture.

The ancestral home of the Thanes of Cawdor – the reputed setting for Duncan's murder in Shakespeare's *Macbeth* – traces its roots back to William, the fourteenth-century thane, a supporter of Robert the Bruce. The importance of its historical setting is paramount for Cawdor Castle's current custodian, Czech-born Angelika, Dowager Countess of Cawdor, whose self-confessed lack of gardening knowledge has been fully compensated for by her understanding of colour, shape, and form, and her attention to detail.

SYMBOLIC SPACES

Passionate about history and conservation, Lady Cawdor has created gardens full of symbolism. In the eighteenth-century formal Flower Garden, she has added the Slate Garden, a saltire-shaped space that pays homage to the solar system, with blue, white, and yellow plants. The spherical fountain, by Kirkcaldy-based artist James Parker, uses recycled slates from the castle roof to represent the sun, while the moon is represented by a crescent-shaped slate bench.

Next is the sixteenth-century Walled Garden, with its spectacular Labyrinth of trained holly, a pyramid shape at the centre, as well as a statue of the Minotaur by American artist Gregory Ryan. Spring colour comes from the yellow laburnum tunnel on three sides and a golden autumn blast from espaliered field maples.

Tucked behind it are more symbolic gardens, loosely divided into four distinct spaces. In the Paradise Garden, planted in pale shades to create peace, there is something in flower all year. The Knot Garden is planted with seventeenth-century herbs and medicinal plants, while Purgatory is symbolized by prickly plants, mainly thistles. The Garden of Eden is, of course, evoked by fruit trees.

The crescendo is reached in Arabella Lennox-Boyd's Long Border, along the west-facing wall, with its blast of late-summer colour drawn from the 1810 book *Theory of Colours* by Johann Wolfgang von Goethe. Green foliage soothes and calms, yellow hemerocallis give out positive vibes and orange lilies joy, while pops of red bring intensity – a mix of sensations that together encapsulate the experience of Cawdor.

Clockwise from right
The laburnum tunnel underplanted with self-sown Welsh poppies.

The focal point of the Slate Garden is the fountain by James Parker.

The ancient towers of Cawdor Castle rise above the Flower Garden.

FOCUS ON

Auchindoune

A walk through the Cawdor Big Wood leads to Auchindoune. This wild garden beside the Cawdor burn was first planted in 1925, with plants brought back by Jack Cawdor, 23rd Thane, from his expedition to the Tsangpo gorge in Tibet with plant collector Frank Kingdon-Ward. More recently, garden designer Arabella Lennox-Boyd was commissioned to lay out the vegetable garden, which is cultivated on biodynamic principles with emphasis on soil health and wildlife.

FOCUS ON

The Amphitheatre

A spectacular open-air sunken amphitheatre is part of Arne Maynard's original design as a space for bringing the local community together in the garden. The cosy atmosphere lends itself well to theatre and concert events, to which people are invited to bring picnics.

Clockwise from above right *Mown paths form a grass maze, with the geometric beds and holiday cottage behind.*

Poppy seed heads float above the blue flowers of Catananche caerulea*.*

Michaelmas Red apples, one of 60 varieties grown in the Fruit Gardens.

Gordon Castle Walled Garden

WHERE *Fochabers, Moray, IV32 7PQ* WHEN *Year round: spring for bulbs; summer for flowers, vegetables, and herbs; autumn for fruit; winter for structure* WHAT *One of Britain's largest kitchen gardens at 3.2 hectares (8 acres), restored with the help of designer Arne Maynard*

In 2008, Zara and Angus Gordon Lennox, descendants of the dukes of Gordon and current custodians of the Gordon Castle estate, began a major restoration of the historic but neglected Walled Garden, with the aim of reviving its productive past.

The restoration of Gordon Castle's Walled Garden got off to an unpromising start. The first designer Zara and Angus approached took one look at the 262 espaliered apple trees remaining in the otherwise grassed-over space and commented: "You must be barking mad."

Fortunately, Bath-based designer Arne Maynard shared the couple's vision to create a productive and beautiful garden based on a mix of fruit trees, vegetables, and fragrant herb and cut-flower beds. He understood their desire to produce their own gin using botanicals such as mint and lavender, and to make liquors with fruit grown in the garden.

A WALLED MARVEL

Structurally, the focal point of the garden is the old head gardener's eighteenth-century house (now a holiday cottage), built into the south garden wall, which aligns with the original gates and paths. Flowing from here, Maynard's design is an elegant, geometric layout of 12 vegetable and annual beds, divided by brick-edged paths radiating from a central lavender-enclosed pond. Colour-themed in white, red, yellow, pink, and blue, the plants include nigella, marigolds, dahlias, and roses, merging with long rows of sweet peas and perennials. Groups of purple salvia link drifts of chives, rosemary, purple sage, and thyme, punctuated with white valerian. All produce is used in the house, café, and shop.

Natural year-round structure comes from arches of pears and paths lined with fruit trees espaliered on iron rods and rows of step-over apples: many Scottish varieties feature in the 742 newly planted fruit trees. Quirky elements include a grass maze, a 400-seat sunken amphitheatre, and a natural children's play area assembled from "old bits of the original castle". The Victorian glasshouses have also been skilfully restored by estate workers.

A particular joy is the sensory elements of the garden: the fragrance of the herb beds edged with cloud-pruned rosemary, the hum of bees on the lavender, and the birds, including oystercatchers, which flourish in this space.

Top *Veronicastrum drifts fill a border of the Upper Terrace.*

Bottom *The formal box parterre featuring the Seton of Pitmedden arms.*

Pitmedden Garden

WHERE *Ellon, Aberdeenshire, AB41 7PD* WHEN *Late spring, summer, and early autumn for the inspirational planting* WHAT *A classical layout of parterres with formal planting contrasting with a naturalist design by Chris Beardshaw*

Hidden in rural Aberdeenshire but influenced by landscape architect André Le Nôtre's seventeenth-century designs for Vaux-le-Vicomte and Versailles, Pitmedden delivers a powerful surprise: a combination of horticulture, history, and contemporary planting.

Nothing quite prepares you for your first glimpse of the four formal terraces of Pitmedden, bearing all the hallmarks of classical design below the modest Georgian house.

Designed in the late 1600s by Sir Alexander Seton, the garden almost certainly benefited from the skills of architect William Bruce of Kinross. Widely credited with introducing classical architecture to Scotland, Bruce was influenced by French and Italian architecture, so the terraces are enclosed by tall stone walls strewn with roses or espaliered apples, and embellished with pavilions, a fountain, and a central yew *allée*. An astonishing 5 miles (8km) of box hedges edge the geometric parterres.

The National Trust for Scotland acquired Pitmedden in 1952 when an awareness of the importance of landscape history inspired a reimagining of the original, lost designs. Seeking ideas, the Trust found a plan of the parterres at Holyroodhouse – also designed by Bruce for Charles II – which inspired three of the formal parterres at on the lower terrace, known as the Lion, the Daisy, and the Tempus Fugit. The fourth features the evocative Seton of Pitmedden coat of arms surrounded by the family mottos intricately sculpted from box and framed by the thistle and saltire symbols.

A MODERN PARTERRE

While the blocks of colour in the formal parterre create a major impact, the current star of this show is the Beardshaw-designed parterre on the top terrace. Laid out in 2022, this naturalistic meadow scheme captivates with its drifts of purple, pink, yellow, and blue perennials.

Standout varieties include spiky, blue eryngium; pink cow parsley; *Chaerophyllum hirsutum* 'Roseum', loved by hoverflies; tall, yellow *Phlomis russeliana*, as beautiful in winter as in summer, and red and yellow achillea. The purple *Aster × frikartii* 'Mönch' plays its part in autumn, while scarlet *Helenium* 'Moerheim Beauty' is a captivating beauty indeed.

The latest phase of Pitmedden's restoration, this parterre is alive with insects. Head gardener Lewis Swales often counts as many as 10 different butterflies and hoverflies feeding on the plants.

"Morning is my favourite time when you can hear the buzz and the hum of insects. It feels very natural."

LEWIS SWALES, HEAD GARDENER

Top *The old dovecote is one of the garden's most recognizable features.*

Bottom *The Fountain Garden, with its clipped hedges and Portuguese laurels, has a Victorian feel.*

Crathes Castle Garden

WHERE *Banchory, Aberdeenshire, AB31 5QJ* WHEN *All year round, but most colourful in summer* WHAT *Lavish walled garden divided into "rooms", plus a woodland garden*

The magnificent Walled Garden of this sixteenth-century castle is one of the finest in Scotland. Its layout and its many choice plants arrived in the early twentieth century, but other elements of the garden are much older.

Thanks to a moist and mild microclimate, as well as fertile soil, delicate plants flourish here at the 400-year-old Walled Garden at Crathes Castle. Originally a productive area to provide food for the kitchens of the handsome pink-harled castle, the northern half had by the Victorian era become ornamental gardens.

The current layout, established by Sir James and Lady Burnett during the twentieth century, is split into eight areas, employing impressive yew hedges that in late summer are spangled with the scarlet blooms of scrambling *Tropaeolum speciosum* (flame flower).

Dividing the area into quarters are the famed White Borders, overflowing in summer with perfumed philadelphus, feathery aruncus, and icy hydrangeas, and double herbaceous border, which glows with colour into autumn. In the centre is a venerable mushroom-pruned Portuguese laurel, thought to be 200 years old. Don't miss the Golden Garden, the June Borders with their massed displays of lupins and oriental poppies and views of the old dovecote, and the glasshouses where a collection of historic Malmaison carnations can be enjoyed.

EVER CHANGING

Recent years have seen a wealth of changes. Visitors today enter the garden via the timber-framed Welcome Building with its sedum roof, while the Rose Garden has been redesigned with a circular layout. Here, modern rose cultivars mingle with lavender, grasses, and agapanthus in a drought-, pest-, and disease-resistant combination, replacing earlier schemes.

The theme of change continues in the new, triangular Evolution Garden, planted with ferns, horsetails, and the unusual tree *Trochodendron aralioides*. Venture outside the walls to enjoy the Woodland Garden, the collection of historic daffodils, and the "egg and egg cup" yews, thought to be almost as old as the castle itself.

FOCUS ON

A Perfect Partnership

From around 1926, Sir James and Lady Burnett shaped the gardens we now see at Crathes. Sir James was interested in trees and shrubs, and his friendship with Sir Harold Hillier (see page 100) resulted in plantings of rare species. His wife, Sybil, a highly regarded plantswoman, was fascinated by herbaceous plants and how best to combine them.

Scone Palace

WHERE *Perth, PH2 6BD* WHEN *Best from March until October, but also in February for snowdrops* WHAT *A 40.5-hectare (100-acre) garden described as "one giant woodland with pockets of formal planting"*

The site of a Roman encampment, a Pictish capital, and Robert the Bruce's coronation in 1306, with links to renowned plant collectors, Scone Palace and its gardens are steeped in 2,000 years of Scottish history.

Current owners of Scone Lord and Lady Mansfield have a passion for its history, while ensuring they remain at the forefront of Scottish gardening. The lands around the abbey that once stood here were first tended 900 years ago by Augustinian monks, but when the abbey was sacked during the Reformation the site passed to the Murray family.

Today, designed to be of year-round interest, the woodland garden is threaded with mown paths winding through a dazzling spring display of rhododendrons and fragrant yellow azaleas. In autumn, summer greens give way to the vibrant reds, yellows, and golds of, among others, a growing collection of acers.

WOODLAND WONDERLAND

Trees are key to the garden, with oaks, beeches, and a sycamore planted by James VI and I in 1617 taking pride of place. The Woodland Garden was inspired by the 3rd Earl, who, in 1804, hired John Claudius Loudon to develop the grounds. A highlight of the conifer collection is a champion Douglas fir grown from seed gathered by plant collector David Douglas.

The morning air in the Victorian Pinetum is fresh with the scent of pine needles. A natural extension to the Woodland Garden, it was planted in the 1840s by the 4th Earl, who took advantage of exciting new introductions to assemble a rare collection of hemlocks, noble firs, and sequoias.

EYE-CATCHING ORNAMENT

The contemporary Murray Maze, designed by Adrian Fisher, sits on the site of the ancient Monk's Playgreen. Its 800 metres (2,625ft) of pathways are made of over 2,000 copper and green beech trees, inspired by the family tartan.

Flowers and vegetables are produced in the Victorian Walled Garden, currently the subject of an ambitious restoration project, including the creation of the formal Lady Mansfield Garden tucked behind a lime-tree hedge set against a foreground of *Verbena bonariensis*.

In late winter drifts of snowdrops run up the old drive to the palace, and in the woods is a small display of *Galanthus plicatus* brought back by estate workers from the Crimean War. Visit in mid-February to see them at their best.

Clockwise from right
Scone is famed for its champion Douglas firs in the Arboretum.

The Murray Maze is planted with copper and green beech in the shape of a five-pointed star.

Deer sculptures stand sentry before the palace.

FOCUS ON

David Douglas

The son of a Scone stonemason, botanist and plant collector David Douglas (1799–1834) started working in the garden as a child. He displayed a talent and enthusiasm that brought him to the attention of the Botanical Gardens of Glasgow and the RHS. Taking part in numerous expeditions to the Pacific Northwest, he is best known for introducing the Douglas fir to Scotland.

FOCUS ON

Daffodils

During daffodil season, visitors to Backhouse Rossie can see the development of the first British polyploid cultivars, which changed daffodil breeding around the world forever, alongside breathtaking varieties with pink or red coronas. Aptly, the gardens also play host to Scotland's annual Daffodil Festival in April.

Backhouse Rossie Estate

WHERE *Fife, KY15 7UZ* WHEN *April to September* WHAT *A historic estate renowned for its national collection of daffodils and Scotland's longest rose archway*

The Backhouse Rossie Estate, which dates back to the eleventh century, is set within a historic landscape with views to the Lomond Hills. Having bought it in 2005, Caroline and Andrew Thomson are restoring and building on their ancestors' unique horticultural legacy.

Left *'Direktör Benschop' roses flower above the double helix of the DNA Pathway.*

Far left *The double flowers of* Narcissus *'Glowing Phoenix'.*

Caroline Thomson is a direct descendant of the Quaker Backhouse family, whose interests were in ethical banking and botany. In 1815, brothers James and Thomas Backhouse co-founded the Backhouse Nursery of York, which by the late 1800s was larger than Kew Gardens, employing over 110 people. When the nursery closed in 1955 and the land was turned into a public park, the Backhouse family legacy was in danger of being lost, but their dream is now revived at Backhouse Rossie.

While Andrew shouldered the task of restoring the rundown house and estate, Caroline researched archive materials, seeking to locate the disappearing plants bred by three generations of the Backhouse family over the nineteenth and twentieth centuries – particularly their groundbreaking cultivars of *Narcissus*. In 2016, this collection numbered 82 and was awarded National Plant Collection status.

SCIENCE AND NATURE

The restored Walled Garden is the heart of the estate, and is themed around art and science, in keeping with the Backhouse family's history of botanical innovation. Visitors enter through an oak door, where Scotland's longest rose archway dissects the 0.5 hectares (1¼ acres) east to west. It is smothered by scented *Rosa* 'Direktör Benschop', with its semi-double white flowers in summer. Below the archway, the DNA Pathway, its reclaimed cobbles laid in a double-helix design, leads to relaxed herbaceous and rose plantings surrounding a centromere-shaped sculpture.

Double yew-backed herbaceous borders divide the garden north to south, where *Lavandula angustifolia* 'Backhouse Purple', introduced in 1888 as the first named deep-purple cultivar, grows in clay pots beside the water feature. A Backhouse *Penstemon* 'Newbury Gem' thrives in the parterre quarter, with its *Buxus*-lined beds of scented herbs and ornamental cut flowers. *Correa backhouseana*, a half-hardy shrub with whiteish tubular flowers, grows in the Victorian glasshouse, while *Malus domestica* 'Flower of the Town' grows alongside old espalier pears, plums, and quince. Scottish apples grow around the perimeter walls, and in the fourth quarter lies a medieval-inspired grass Labyrinth, surrounded by alliums that pop with colour in spring.

In late summer, the contemporary perennial plantings in the Walled Garden are one of many highlights at Cambo.

Cambo

WHERE *Kingsbarns, St Andrews, Fife, KY16 8QD* WHEN *Year-round interest; late winter for snowdrops; summer for the Walled Garden* WHAT *A stunning Georgian walled garden with modern, naturalistic plantings of perennials, a Woodland Walk, and Winter Garden featuring a diverse collection of snowdrops*

Just 7 miles (11km) south of St Andrews on the East Coast of Scotland, around an hour's drive from Edinburgh, lies Cambo, a 486-hectare (1,200-acre) estate that has been home to the Erskine family for over 300 years. It is renowned for its beautifully planted, 1-hectare (2.5-acre) Walled Garden, inspired by the naturalistic perennial meadow style.

Set within sight of the late-Victorian house, the Walled Garden at Cambo dates from the earlier Georgian period and is the focal point of the garden. It is both remarkable and unusual, as it was constructed around a stream – the Cambo Burn – which meanders from north to south through the centre, and even includes a small waterfall. Bridges cross it here and there, providing a distinctive feel, and eventually it flows out under the walls to the sea beyond.

As spring arrives, dazzling displays of tulips bloom within the Walled Garden; Cambo even runs a Tulip Festival in May. If you visit towards the end of spring, enjoy the deliciously fragrant Lilac Walk, which includes more than 20 different selections. At this time of year the garden's massed displays of alliums will also be reaching their peak. The extensive rose collection, with more than 200, often highly fragrant selections on show, is not to be missed either.

With its contemporary plantings of perennials, and its ornamental potager that stylishly mixes annuals, perennials, and vegetables, the Walled Garden is sublime throughout summer and autumn. Delights include spectacular double herbaceous borders with dazzling naturalistic drifts of perennials such as *Monarda*, *Sanguisorba*, *Helenium*, and *Eryngium*, blending with swaying grasses such as *Stipa* and *Miscanthus*. These combinations remain effective right through into November, when the structural seedheads of many plants come to the fore. In August, September, and October another marvellous area is the North American Prairie Garden, which abounds with asters and *Echinacea*.

From left to right
Hardy fuchsias enjoy the moist, mild conditions by the Cambo Burn.

Cambo's famous snowdrops grow in the Winter Garden and the estate's woodland.

Perfumed sweet peas are a summer favourite in the Walled Garden.

SNOWDROP SPECTACULAR

In late winter, the snowdrops at Cambo are a particular sensation; they pop up everywhere, for they are one of the garden's great specialities. Evidence of the first plantings at Cambo can be traced all the way back to 1801, but the collection took off in earnest in the 1930s, when Lady Magdalen Erskine encouraged *Galanthus nivalis* to naturalize in the woodland, dividing and replanting bulbs. Then, in the 1980s, Lady Catherine Erskine began selling them via mail order, greatly expanding the collection.

Today, the garden holds a Plant Heritage National Plant Collection of around 300 different selections, seen at their best during the Scottish Snowdrop Festival, which runs from late January to early March, drawing in galanthophiles from near and far. At this time of year, masses of snowdrops line the main driveway to the house and fill the Woodland Walk around the burn as it winds out to the sea. Many of the more sophisticated species can be found gracing Cambo's beautiful Winter Garden, either as the underplanting to glistening multi-stemmed birch trees, vibrant stems of *Cornus*, and various winter-flowering shrubs, or combining with hellebores, wintergreen bergenia, black-leaved *Ophiopogon*, and *Epimedium*.

A GARDEN FOR ALL SEASONS

It's hard to pick the best time of year for a visit to Cambo; it has something wonderful to offer in every season. Summer is spectacular, and the Winter Garden and Woodland Walk to the coast, dotted with naturalized snowdrops, daffodils, primroses, and other spring-flowering bulbs, from aconites to wild garlic, ensure that a visit is rewarding at any time of year. But on a sunny February day, take the Woodland Walk to Kingsbarns Beach, when the sight of massed snowdrops under trees with sand dunes just beyond combines with the salty air and the sound of breaking waves for a moment that lives long in the memory.

GARDEN INSPIRATION

Snowdrops

The process of naturalizing snowdrops can take several years, but there are steps you can take to encourage them. Plant the bulbs in a part-shaded area, in loose clusters, and let the leaves die back after flowering to replenish the bulbs. After a few years, divide and replant established clumps to help them spread. *Galanthus nivalis* is particularly prone to naturalizing.

TIMELINE OF EVENTS

1668

Sir Charles Erskine buys Cambo; the estate eventually passes out of the family.

1790s

The estate is rebought by Thomas Erskine, 9th Earl of Kellie, who makes improvements and adds the current walled garden.

1801

The first snowdrops are planted by the 9th Earl.

1878

The house is destroyed by fire; a new house is completed in 1881.

1933

Gardens are opened to the public.

1976

Peter and Catherine Erskine begin reviving Cambo and its Walled Garden.

1980s

The woodland is cleared to allow snowdrops to flourish.

2007

The Scottish Snowdrop Festival is started at Cambo by Catherine Erskine.

Shepherd House Garden

WHERE *Inveresk, Midlothian, EH21 7TH* WHEN *February for snowdrops; May for tulips; summer for roses; autumn for foliage* WHAT *A triangular-shaped walled garden, widely regarded as the jewel in the crown of small Scottish gardens*

The immaculate parterre in front of Shepherd House, home of Sir Charles and Lady Ann Fraser, is the perfect foil for the treasures hidden in the garden behind, where a display of theatrical architectural elements unfolds against vibrant year-round planting.

Shepherd House is as much the story of a partnership as it is the story of the garden. For over six decades, the 0.4-hectare (1-acre) plot has evolved from a combination of Ann Fraser's artistic talents and Charles Fraser's ability to interpret and execute a flow of ideas while keeping the garden in perfect order.

ROMANTIC PLANTING

Behind the house is the Millennium Garden, where geometric box beds are planted with Ann's favourite tulips, irises, and poppies – all inspiring subjects for her botanical paintings. The centre of the garden is defined by a rill, inspired by a visit to the Alhambra palace in Spain, which runs between two ponds via a wide grass path edged with alliums and *Nepeta* 'Six Hills Giant'. In summer, arches smothered with rambling white roses 'Bobbie James', 'Wedding Day', and 'Seagull' cast dappled shade.

As with the front parterre, the inspiration for Charles's vegetable garden came from Rosemary Verey's iconic garden at Barnsley House in Gloucestershire. Here, vegetables are produced in raised beds by the Potting Shed, with its living roof, in much-loved straight lines.

A quarter of the garden is laid out as an informal woodland with trees, including *Magnolia* 'Elizabeth', *Prunus serrula*, the Japanese Pagoda tree *Styphnolobium japonicum*, and reliable, spring-flowering *Cornus* 'Eddie's White Wonder'. In the small bulb and wildflower meadow, crocuses and fritillaries give way to cowslips and *Tulipa* 'Queen of Night'.

SETTING THE SCENE

With an eye for theatricality, the Frasers soon added an ornamental sheep fank (Scots for sheep's pen), followed by the Shell House. Other architectural features include the sculpture *Girl Washing Her Hair* by the late Gerald Laing at the lower pond, the sundial over the garden door, a bronze resin cockerel, and a dry-stone spiral seat by Nigel Bialy. "The process is the purpose," says Charles. "We find the most exciting thing about the garden is planning the next project."

Clockwise from top left *Bearded Iris 'Beverly Sills', chosen to match the colour of Shell House.*

Scallop, limpet, and mussel shells were used to decorate the walls of the Shell House.

A loose colour scheme of blue, pink, and white informs the planting of the Millennium Parterre.

Right *The aviary fits neatly into the courtyard garden's chequerboard design.*

Below *Garden forks feature in the Kitchen and Cutting Garden gate.*

GARDEN INSPIRATION

Beauty in Repetition

In his previous East Lothian garden, Rob noticed how a pairing of *Cotinus coggygria* 'Royal Purple' and *Euphorbia wallichii* looked good for an exceptionally long period. "It was an easy thing to repeat this, alternating them down the longest bed in the garden – a narrow south-facing strip against the house." The same principles have been applied to the Thug Bed in the Lower Courtyard.

Broadwoodside

WHERE *Gifford, East Lothian, EH41 4JQ* WHEN *Year round for the structure*
WHAT *A classical design interpreted along simple, contemporary lines with quirky twists*

In 1997, when Robert Dalrymple was persuaded by his wife Anna to look at Broadwoodside, he found a derelict farm steading among fields of wheat. It was the "beautiful outlook and the buildings' potential" that convinced him of what it could be.

With the help of Edinburgh architect Nicholas Groves-Raines, Rob and Anna began to plan the garden that had started to form in their mind's eye. For Rob, a book designer, the articulation of a two-dimensional space came easily. Much harder was the planting. "To get a group of plants to give a pleasing display over successive seasons, and from one year to the next, is a demanding skill," he says. Happily, gardener Guy Donaldson took over and, on his retirement, Nanette Wraith.

ELEGANT SIMPLICITY

The heart of the garden is the Upper Courtyard, where the aim was for green structure that would look good during the long Scottish winters. The answer was a chequerboard design, with eight square beds planted with a single contrasting evergreen: yew and box, germander speedwell, pachysandra, purple-flowering *Ophiopogon bodinieri*, the grass *Seslaria autumnalis*, rosemary, and box balls. A wooden aviary in the centre of the courtyard is home to William, the grey African parrot, while the south-facing courtyard byre was opened up to create a covered entertaining area. Furnished with a slate tank and terracotta pots, the effect is "surprisingly Italianate for southern Scotland". A perimeter border in the Lower Courtyard – described by Rob as a "Thug Bed" – is where *Macleaya cordata*, *Eutrochium purpureum*, and Japanese anemones "have been slugging it out for more than twenty years", to great effect.

Outside of the courtyards, a flagstone path leads to the ochre-washed old farmhouse. The walkway is flanked on either side by pollarded limes and box balls underplanted with a naturalistic palette of aquilegia, brunnera, and *Euphorbia polychroma*. In the Walled Garden to the south, cutting flowers and vegetables are grown in raised beds, and mixed borders flank a rectangular pond fed from rainwater.

Beyond the steading, grass paths lead through the orchard and informal woodland, punctuated with quirky sculptures, including a trio of apples, each one progressively bitten into. An old lime avenue leads to the Temple, the Victorian portico salvaged from Strathleven House, Dunbartonshire, when it was restored – one of a number of follies and installations within the farmland that make a stroll around Broadwoodside inspirational all year round.

The hot borders in high summer, leading to the Head Gardener's Cottage.

Floors Castle

WHERE *Kelso, Roxburghshire, TD5 7SF* WHEN *April to September; all year for the grounds and River Tweed walks; February for snowdrops* WHAT *Expansive castle grounds centring on a magnificent Victorian Walled Garden*

Floors Castle sits in a raised position overlooking the River Tweed and the Borders Abbey town of Kelso. The 1.6-hectare (4-acre) Victorian Walled Garden, renowned for its exuberant herbaceous borders and vegetable garden, sits in the heart of the parkland.

Built in 1721 for the 1st Duke of Roxburghe and now home to the 11th Duke and his family, Floors Castle is linked to the Walled Garden by the woodland Star Plantation. Here, grass paths radiate past wildflower-filled glades towards the contrasting Millennium Garden, an elegant French-style gravel-and-grass parterre punctuated with fruit trees.

PRIZE BORDERS

Laid out in a traditional Scottish cruciform style, the Walled Garden perfectly showcases its dazzling herbaceous borders. The impact is immediate: flanked by oversized terracotta containers and set opposite a long river of blue agapanthus, the east-to-west Blue and Silver Border is a glorious blend of eryngiums, *Thalictrum* 'Elin', *Verbena bonariensis*, and silvery *Onopordum acanthium*. Height comes from tall birch tripods smothered in *Clematis* 'Praecox'.

Overlooked by the old Head Gardener's Cottage is the contrasting north-to-south Hot Border, with a fiery selection of inula, deep-red helenium, orange alstroemeria, *Achillea* 'Terracotta', *Lychnis chalcedonica*, and kniphofia. Tucked in between is the Tapestry Garden, designed by Jim Marshall, former gardens adviser to the National Trust, with input from Angel Collins. Here, grass paths wind informally between beds planted in soft, muted colours, inspired by the tapestries in the castle. Natural structure comes from white-barked *Betula utilis* subsp. *jacquemontii*, tall umbellifers, domes of pink lychnis, spires of purple salvia, and mounds of different geraniums.

Dividing the garden horizontally, the parallel summer borders feature rivers of blue veronicastrum, dark-blue aconitum, tall, white, fluffy *Aruncus dioicus*, airy *Crambe cordifolia*, and pale yellow *Cephalaria gigantea*, enveloping you in colour, texture, and form. Scent comes from roses, including the deep-pink *Rosa* 'American Pillar', smothering arches and pyramids.

In the vegetable garden, heritage varieties are cultivated to supply the castle and cafés, while the cutting garden is planted with annuals; like the borders, it always attracts insects. Along the west wall, peony, delphinium, ginger lily, and dahlia beds succeed each other, the latter alternating with stunning tulips in spring.

Clockwise from top left
A striking combination of Echinacea purpurea *'Green Twister' and* Lysimachia.

Completed in 2014, the Belvedere rises above the Queen Elizabeth Walled Garden.

On the main terrace, a box and yew parterre frames a fountain by William Pye.

FOCUS ON

A Royal Passion Project

Everything at Dumfries House reflects the King's vision and his attention to detail. "He is interested in everything, listens, and offers guidance," explains Melissa Simpson, head of horticulture since 2020. "He is a very good artist and will comment on different areas." Wildlife and pollinators are at the forefront of plant choices. "We are keen to see how we can improve nature while keeping it interesting from a horticulture point of view."

Dumfries House

WHERE *Cumnock, Ayrshire, KA18 2NJ* WHEN *All year round*
WHAT *A 243-hectare (600-acre) garden and designed landscape including a variety of diverse gardens set among historic and traditionally constructed new buildings*

Dumfries House sits at the heart of an 809-hectare (2,000-acre) mixed arable and woodland estate. In 2007, His Majesty King Charles III launched a dramatic appeal to save the house and land from sale at auction, with the aim of restoring it as a valued local amenity.

King Charles turned his attention to the gardens in 2012, introducing educational and training opportunities for traditional skills and crafts. Dumfries House is now headquarters of the King's Foundation. The King's vision for the garden is perfectly encapsulated by the spectacular William Pye pergola fountain in front of the house. The jets of water flowing down four arches into bronze pools offer a fascinating glimpse into the workings of hydraulic pressure.

On either side, rose-filled box parterres give way to yew mazes, inspired by a similar pairing enjoyed by the King as a child at Sandringham, while a romantic profusion of wisteria and clematis scrambles up the front of the house.

EDUCATION AND INNOVATION

The route to the Walled Garden leads past the Rothesay Garden, a Japanese-style space complete with a tea house, 4.8 hectares (12 acres) of developing woodland, and the original laundry – now the Royal Drawing School. The King's passion for trees is clear in the Arboretum, where paths radiate from a central octagonal shelter, built by the King's Foundation students. The graceful John Adam-designed bridge over the Lugar Water offers an early glimpse of another octagonal building, the Gothic-style Belvedere Building on the upper terrace of the Walled Garden. Designed by the King, this striking red-brick summerhouse rises above a theatrical layout of terraces, parterres, vegetable beds, and glasshouses.

The Walled Garden is loosely divided into three spaces, the first of which takes its semi-formal cue from the Belvedere, with its backdrop of yew topiary. At the far end, the Pierburg Building overlooks the Kauffman Education Garden, an organic vegetable and perennial garden, where children can follow the process of sowing, composting, picking, and cooking. The fragrance of hundreds of roses hits you in the Rose Garden – thought to be one of the largest in Scotland – with varieties selected for their repeat flowering and fragrance. Nearby is the ancient sycamore planted in 1599 during the reign of James VI, rescued by King Charles with the help of a tree surgeon. The garden's remit is to educate and inspire visitors – and it certainly does that.

From the lake there are magnificent views to the Mull of Galloway and the Isle of Man.

Glenwhan Gardens & Arboretum

WHERE *Dunragit, Stranraer, Wigtownshire, DG9 8PH* WHEN *Year-round interest*
WHAT *A rugged hillside garden with an arboretum and an 8-hectare (20-acre) Moorland Walk*

Winding paths encourage exploration of this hillside garden clawed from wild moorland by Tessa Knott-Sinclair since 1974. Discover a pair of bird-friendly lochans, a water garden, 1,000 rhododendrons and hydrangeas, rare trees, and bluebells in the Moorland Walk.

In 1971, Tessa and her late husband, Bill Knott, bought 42 hectares (103 acres) of windswept, waterlogged moorland, "unseen over the telephone". The ruined farmhouse was occupied by cattle and pigeons, and there was no garden. While Bill farmed, Tessa became inspired by visits to nearby Logan Botanic Garden (see page 194) to create her own.

Aware of the warming effects of the Gulf Stream, Tessa fenced off 5 hectares (12 acres) of hillside behind the house and planted a shelterbelt of mixed conifers and hardwoods around the perimeter "to tame the winds". While this matured, she cleared gorse, bracken, and brambles, and started laying out a network of paths. Two lochans were dug, which are fed by the Georgian reservoir above the garden. Now surrounded with iris and birch reflecting in their peaty waters, they are the stars of the show. Tessa also hand-dug the series of ponds above the lochans to create the Water Garden.

Next, she acquired car-loads of plants – propagated from cuttings, grown from seed, and gratefully accepted from friends. The result was 500 rhododendrons and 450 hydrangeas as well as an abundance of other autumn and spring-flowering shrubs. In spring, the Moorland Walk is covered with bluebells – a sign, Tessa explains, that Glenwhan was once the site of an ancient woodland.

WOODLAND WONDERS

Describing herself as "an instinctive gardener", Tessa also established an inner Arboretum, which felt right for the landscape. Here, sorbus, acers, prunus, and betulas combine, taking the area from spring blossom to autumn glory.

The tree trail identifies around 135 types, including Tessa's favourites: the Chinese native *Metasequoia glyptostroboides* 'Emerald Feathers', the architectural *Pinus montezumae*, and *Betula albosinensis* 'Hergest', which is endangered in the wild. Other standouts include the scarlet-berried *Sorbus insignis*, and *Stewartia pseudocamellia*, with its saucer-shaped white flowers. Fragrant eucryphias combine with hydrangeas to extend the astonishing flowering season into an autumn crescendo.

Giant echiums, tree ferns, and palm trees lend the Walled Garden a tropical atmosphere.

FOCUS ON

Keep Your Appointment

Logan is famed among cineastes as a filming location for the 1972 folk-horror classic *The Wicker Man*. The exotic planting provided a perfect backdrop for Lord Summerisle (Christopher Lee) to extol the fecundity of his orchards to a sceptical Sergeant Howie (Edward Woodward). Logan's first curator, Martin Colledge, can be seen tending to a plant in the foreground as Lee and Woodward stroll between the Chusan palms.

Logan Botanic Garden

WHERE *Port Logan, Stranraer, Dumfries and Galloway, DG9 9ND* WHEN *Year round due to the tropical nature of the planting* WHAT *A 5.6-hectare (14-acre) subtropical plant paradise surrounded by water on three sides*

Lined by 400 cabbage palms, the long drive that leads to the Logan Botanic Garden – a satellite of the Royal Botanical Garden Edinburgh since 1969 – creates a major impact straight away. As curator Richard Baines says, "Visitors immediately know they are somewhere special."

Logan sprang to life in 1869, the vision of Agnes Buchan-Hepburn, wife of landowner James McDouall. She experimented with tender, Southern Hemisphere plants suited to the mild, damp climate, and is reputed to have planted the first eucalyptus in Scotland.

In the intervening 150 years the garden has been transformed into a textured antipodean forest of some 2,500 plant species – many of them on the endangered list. Clusters of Chusan palms (*Trachycarpus fortune*) and feathery tree ferns (*Dicksonia antarctica*) stand out.

AN EXOTIC PARADISE

The 1.2-hectare (3-acre) Walled Garden is described by Richard Baines as "a sea of exoticness". Highlights include the rectangular, stone-edged pond, which is home to koi carp and fringed with arum lilies in summer, followed by bubble-pink nerines. Structure comes from established 100-year-old cordylines.

Different banana species are a thrilling find, and gazing up the trunk into the umbrella-shaped fronds of the giant black tree fern *Sphaeropteris medullaris* transports you straight to the south-west Pacific. Another excitement is the rare *Polylepis australis*, with its wildly peeling bark. Unexpectedly, in July, *Rhododendron dalhousieae* var. *rhabdotum* produces exquisite lily-like white blooms with red stripes.

TENDER LOVING CARE

The team at Logan are justly proud of the geographically themed beds, which are alive with colour. In summer, the South African beds glow with orange and red *Watsonia*, pineapple-shaped *Eucomis*, and a ribbon of blue *Salvia concolor* spilling over the pathways. Pink *Camellia sasanqua*, with its bubble-gum fragrance, is an autumn showstopper. The Logan Conservatory is home to a particularly tender range of South African plants, including *Protea neriifolia* and *Iochroma cyaneum*.

In the Woodland Garden, Tasmanian and Chilean species such as southern beeches combine with giant tree ferns and groves of towering gunnera. Agnes's collection of sweet-smelling eucalyptus has expanded throughout.

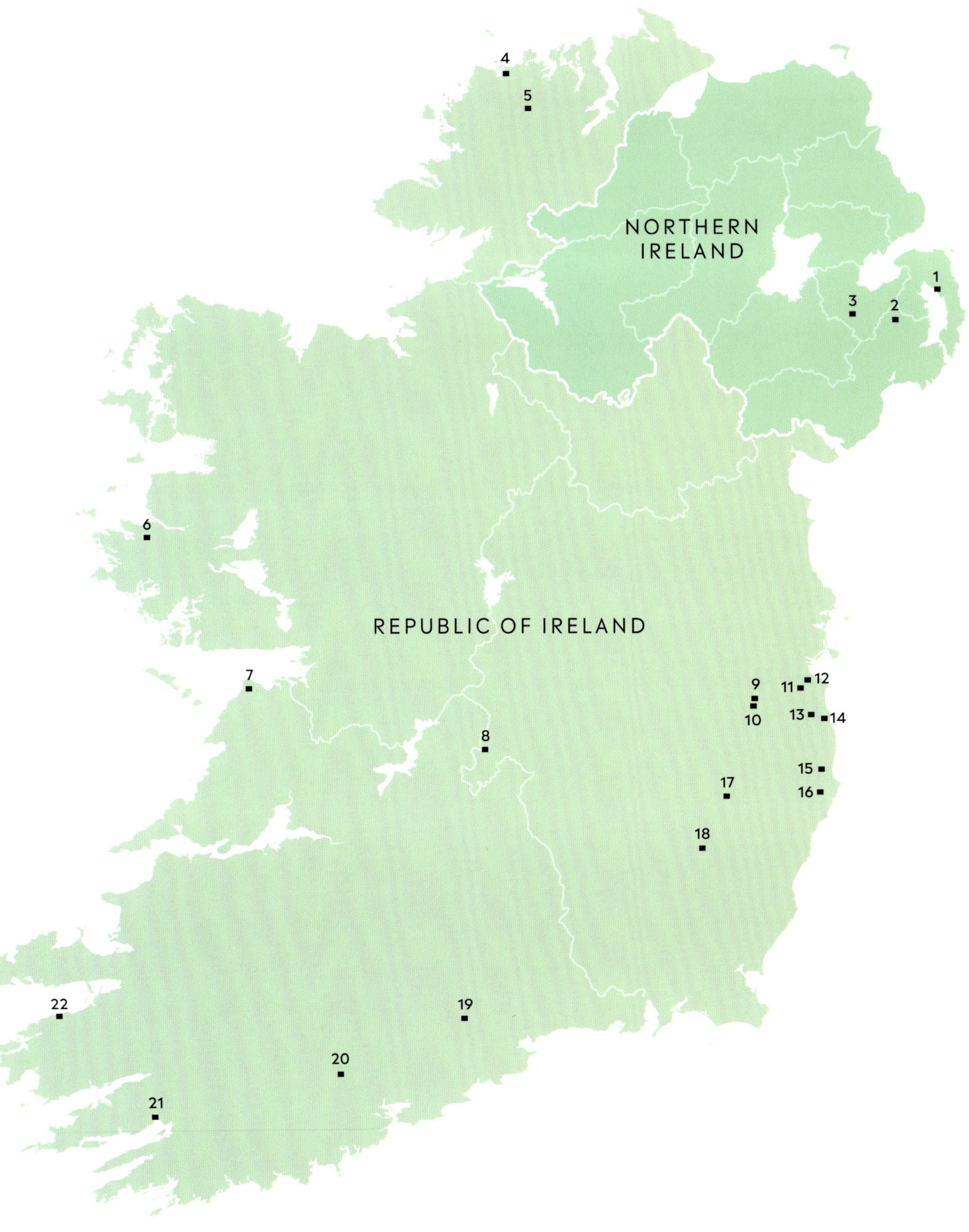
4
5
NORTHERN
IRELAND
1
3
2
6
REPUBLIC OF IRELAND
7
9
11
12
10
13
14
8
15
17
16
18
22
19
20
21

Ireland

Given its temperate, maritime climate and elemental landscape, it's not surprising that Ireland is known worldwide for the beauty and diversity of its gardens. From wonderful historical demesnes to contemporary gems, these exemplify a uniquely Irish approach to the art and craft of garden making that's a glorious fusion of creativity, whimsy, and practicality.

NORTHERN IRELAND

1 MOUNT STEWART HOUSE & GARDENS
2 ROWALLANE GARDEN
3 HILLSBOROUGH CASTLE GARDENS

REPUBLIC OF IRELAND

4 CLUAIN NA DTOR
5 GLENVEAGH CASTLE GARDENS
6 KYLEMORE ABBEY
7 CAHER BRIDGE GARDEN
8 RHSI BELLEFIELD HOUSE & GARDENS
9 HUNTING BROOK GARDENS
10 JUNE BLAKE'S GARDENS
11 DANESMOATE GARDENS
12 AIRFIELD GARDENS
13 POWERSCOURT GARDENS
14 KILRUDDERY HOUSE & GARDENS
15 MOUNT USHER GARDENS
16 NATIONAL BOTANIC GARDENS, KILMACURRAGH
17 PATTHANA GARDENS
18 ALTAMONT GARDENS
19 LISMORE CASTLE GARDENS
20 BLARNEY CASTLE GARDENS
21 ILNACULLIN
22 KELLS BAY

The Sunk Garden, a collaboration with Gertude Jekyll, features a central pool surrounded by beds planted in vivid shades.

Mount Stewart House & Gardens

WHERE *Portaferry Road, Newtownards, County Down, BT22 2AD*
WHEN *Year-round interest* WHAT *An important Irish demesne that makes magnificent use of its mild microclimate*

Located on the famously beautiful Ards Peninsula in County Down in Northern Ireland, where it enjoys a protected microclimate with wonderful views over Strangford Lough, few gardens can equal Mount Stewart's heady blend of grandeur, whimsy, and exoticism.

Much of Mount Stewart's 28 hectares (70 acres) was laid out in the early twentieth century between 1919 and 1927 by its former owner, famous society and political hostess Edith, 7th Marchioness of Londonderry, who first came to live here in 1921 with her husband, politician Charles Stewart Henry Vane-Tempest-Stewart.

A renowned feature is the Sunk Garden, often attributed to Gertrude Jekyll (see page 240), but which in fact owes much to Lady Londonderry, who adapted Miss Jekyll's designs and went her own way entirely with the parterres, pergola, and planting scheme. Pride of place in the adjacent Shamrock Garden is given to a huge topiary Irish harp of clipped yew above a floral representation of the "red hand of Ulster", picked out in scarlet bedding plants.

Beneath the south-facing facade of the house lies Mount Stewart's formal Italian Garden, complete with statuesque pillars topped with mythical gryphons and gods, and its Spanish Garden with its shaded loggia and arcaded hedges. To one side lies the Dodo Terrace, home to an extraordinary collection of elaborate cast-concrete statuary, including gryphons, squirrels, horses, cats, pigs, dinosaurs, and, of course, dodos – a piece of witty satire intended as a fond caricature of family, friends, and various prominent political figures of the era.

LAND OF ETERNAL YOUTH

Lady Londonderry also added the Mairi Garden, named after her youngest daughter, with blue-and-white-themed beds in the shape of a Tudor rose. At a distance from the house is the area known as Tír na nÓg (the land of eternal youth in Celtic mythology), where the family's burial ground is located. A substantial height above the far banks of the garden's large ornamental lake, it enjoys a particularly

"Edith saw the garden as a vehicle for her artistic expression. It's full of iconographic references."

NEIL PORTEOUS, HISTORIC GARDEN CONSULTANT

protected microclimate where tender species flourish, including the New Zealand natives *Metrosideros umbellata* and *Dicksonia squarrosa*; several species of the Southern Hemisphere conifer *Widdringtonia*; and the rare Mediterranean conifer *Tetraclinis articulata*.

Encouraged by experienced gardening friends to take full advantage of Mount Stewart's exceptionally mild microclimate, Lady Londonderry took an exciting and experimental approach to planting her new garden, adding many half-hardy plants such as lapageria, mimosa, yucca, agave, echium, olea, rare Southern Hemisphere species of conifers, tender species of rhododendron, and even a camphor tree. Many flourished, defying the gloomy predictions of the naysayers.

NEW LEASE OF LIFE

In 1955, four years before Lady Londonderry's death, care of Mount Stewart's formal gardens was transferred to the National Trust, which gradually took over as guardian of the rest of the estate over the ensuing decades.

After the restoration of the Grade I-listed, eighteenth-century neoclassical house, work has begun to renew Mount Stewart's late-eighteenth-century Walled Garden, which the National Trust acquired in 2014, along with a further 364 hectares (900 acres) belonging to the original estate. With its Rose Garden now reinstated and its Vinery under restoration, this once highly productive, scented space promises to be so again.

FOCUS ON

Restoration Challenges

Effective conservation of this unique and historically significant garden is a challenge, complicated not only by inevitable financial constraints and a growing range of non-native pests and diseases, but also the substantial threat of climate change. Most immediate is the ongoing risk of storm damage and, as sea levels rise, flooding. Working with the Kassandra Project and its own Ark Project, the team at Mount Stewart now plans "a slow and phased retreat of the garden further into the interior of the estate".

Clockwise from top left

The formal Italian Garden, edged with colonnaded Leyland cypress hedges.

The garden's beautifully sited ornamental lake is surrounded by lush woodland planting.

The family's private burial ground, known as Tír na nÓg, is laid out in the shape of a Celtic cross.

Left *Himalayan poppies are strongly connected with Rowallane.*

Below *Rowallane's distinctive cairns, made of water-smoothed stones.*

Bottom *The flower borders in the Walled Garden, with variegated hostas and aruncus.*

GARDEN INSPIRATION

Himalayan Poppies

Meconopsis × sheldonii 'Slieve Donard', the variety of blue Himalayan poppy long associated with Rowallane as well as the famous Slieve Donard Nursery, is prized for its exceptionally beautiful sky-blue flowers, which appear in May. Only suitable for cool, damp, acidic soil and dappled shade, this hybrid perennial variety is infertile so must be propagated through division in early spring.

Rowallane Garden

WHERE *Saintfield, County Down, BT24 7LH* WHEN *Year-round interest, but particularly in spring* WHAT *A 22-hectare (55-acre) plantsperson's garden, home to a world-famous collection of rhododendrons, azaleas, and other choice woodland species*

Acquired by the National Trust in 1955, and now under the skilful care of head gardener Claire McNally, Rowallane Garden exemplifies a hugely exciting era in the world of horticulture, one where new species and varieties of plants were being introduced into cultivation at a dizzying rate by the great plant hunters of the time.

The grounds of Rowallane were originally laid out by the Reverend John Moore, who purchased what in 1858 was a modest Irish farmhouse, along with 202 hectares (500 acres) of poor, stony, windswept farmland. But it was his nephew Hugh Armytage Moore who turned the garden into a plantsperson's dream.

PLANT HUNTERS' PARADISE

Possessed of a keen plantsman's eye, the latter was good friends with many subscribers to the plant-hunting trips of Frank Kingdon Ward, Ernest Wilson, and George Forrest, including Lionel de Rothschild of Exbury Gardens, who shared with him their portion of the seeds collected. He also sourced plants from many of the great nurseries of his era, including Veitch, Daisy Hill, and Slieve Donard, and selected several rhododendron hybrids, including the compact *R. hanceanum* (Nanum Group).

Today, Rowallane is home to a world-class collection of more than 2,000 rhododendrons and azaleas, along with outstanding specimens of magnolia, camellia, nothofagus, pterocarya, davidia, acer, and desfontainia. Even if you've never heard of the garden, you may have come across one of the many outstanding plants that bear its name, including *Hypericum* 'Rowallane' and *Viburnum plicatum* f. *tomentosum* 'Rowallane'.

In the charming Inner Walled Garden, choice perennials and shrubs grow in generous borders, including hellebore, peony, bergenia, crocosmia, agapanthus, roses, hemerocallis, and the wonderful blue Himalayan poppy, *Meconopsis* × *sheldonii* 'Slieve Donard' (see opposite). In the Outer Walled Garden grows a magnificent specimen of the rare *Magnolia dawsoniana* and another of the golden rain tree, with lace-cap hydrangeas, eucryphias, and the famous scarlet-flowered *Chaenomeles* × *superba* 'Rowallane'.

WILD AT HEART

Another feature of Rowallane is Moore's respect for the natural topography of the site, a guiding principle of Robinsonian gardening (see page 91). The Rock Garden, for instance, was formed simply by clearing the ground to expose parts of the existing bedrock. Rhododendrons and azaleas thrive here in the acidic soil alongside meconopsis, primula, and erythronium. They flourish, too, in the Spring Garden, planted for colourful displays on a memorable scale.

Hillsborough Castle Gardens

WHERE *Hillsborough, County Down, BT26 6TY* WHEN *All year round*
WHAT *An extensive, historic Georgian estate just 20 minutes outside Belfast that has enjoyed a remarkable renaissance under the care of the charity Historic Royal Palaces*

The official residence of the Secretary of State for Northern Ireland as well as the British royal family when in Northern Ireland, Hillsborough Castle and its magnificent, organically managed 40-hectare (100-acre) gardens have been transformed into a world-class attraction over the last decade under the care of the charity Historic Royal Palaces.

In their present incarnation, the gardens date from the mid-eighteenth century, with later additions that include the sunny South Terrace, elegant Greek-revival Temple, and South Parterre.

Originally laid out to mark the Diamond Jubilee of Queen Elizabeth II, the Jubilee Parterre was elegantly reworked in 2016 by designer Catherine FitzGerald. It features topiary yews shaped into King Edward crowns standing sentry over lush flower beds planted in pastel shades, arranged around a small formal pool where a delicate fountain plays. Beyond it are the native Wildflower Meadows that head gardener Claire Woods MBE has brought to life in recent years. A biodiversity hotspot, in summer they're filled with wild orchids and other native species.

ELEGANT EVOLUTION

Nearby is the Granville Rose Garden, a charming mid-twentieth-century addition. Its inner beds are filled with varieties of hybrid tea and climbing roses (these include *Rosa* 'Silver Jubilee' and the 'Northern Ireland Centenary Rose', bred by Dickson Roses), surrounded by beds of herbaceous perennials that include aquilegia, oriental poppy, peony, iris, and hemerocallis.

Looking like something from Lewis Carroll's *Alice's Adventures in Wonderland* is the magical Yew Tree Walk of fastigiate Irish yews (see opposite). South of it lies the Lost Garden; the beautifully situated Lady Alice's Temple, and the Moss Walk, off-bounds to visitors to preserve its delicate carpet of bryophytes. Beyond these lie the Glen, Ice House, Lake, and the Pinetum where a collection of mature coniferous trees grow.

Substantially restored and redesigned, the Georgian Walled Garden sits just west of the castle. Covering 1.6 hectares (4 acres), it's a magnificently productive and lovingly tended place, filled with a huge assortment of fruit, herbs, vegetable beds, cut-flower beds, and a double herbaceous border. Its old espalier pear trees include specimens of *Pyrus communis* 'Pitmaston Duchess' and 'Dr Jules Guyot', while heritage apple varieties include 'Ecklinville', 'Kilkenny Pearmain', and 'Ballyfatten'.

GARDEN INSPIRATION

The Irish Yew

Known as the Irish yew or Florence Court yew and grown all over the world, *Taxus baccata* 'Fastigiata' was first discovered by chance in 1740 by a farmer called George Willis, who found it growing near the historic demesne of Florence Court in Fermanagh. Unlike the more spreading species, this evergreen coniferous tree has a very vertical growing habit that makes it a wonderfully dramatic "punctuation" plant, often used to line a formal walkway or mark an entrance.

Top *The famous Yew Tree Walk of Irish yews, framing a distant view of Lady Alice's Temple.*

Bottom *The Jubilee Parterre, with the castle and its South Terrace in the background.*

Cluain na dTor

WHERE *Ballyconnell, Falcarragh, County Donegal, F92H 5W8* WHEN *From mid-summer through to late autumn* WHAT *A contemporary 2-hectare (5-acre) seaside garden created by a brilliant plantsman and nature lover*

That a garden of such exceptional natural beauty has been made so close to the Atlantic coastline is genuinely remarkable. But then so is Cluain na dTor's owner and creator, the nurseryman, garden designer, and botanist Seamus O'Donnell.

The 7 hectares (17 acres) of wet, peaty land on which Cluain na dTor is situated have been in Seamus's family since the 1920s. Inspired by his observations of plants' wild habitats during his own extensive travels as a freshly qualified botanist through Mexico, Costa Rica, South Africa, Australia, New Zealand, and Indonesia in the late 1980s, Seamus began to establish a plant nursery here, specializing in species suitable for exposed coastal conditions. Now, Cluain na dTor is home to a nursery and biodiverse gardens that combine his vast knowledge with an experimental, painterly approach to garden-making.

MICROCLIMATE MARVELS

Warmed by the Gulf Stream, Cluain na dTor is sheltered by mature windbreaks strategically positioned by Seamus, using salt- and wind-tolerant species such as olearia, hebe, willow, sycamore, Sitka spruce, and *Sorbus intermedia*. Within that protected microclimate grows an outstanding selection of plants. Many are Southern Hemisphere plants, chosen not only for their handsome foliage and silhouettes, but also their suitability for the damp, acidic soil.

In the Exotic Garden, schefflera, tetrapanax, brassaiopsis, and restio, as well as palms, bamboos, honey myrtles, and tulip trees, create a tall, leafy canopy. Beneath them, a pebble path wends its way past ferns, ornamental grasses, banana plants, cannas, dahlias, and the ornamental ginger *Cautleya robusta*.

In the Bird Garden, a striking sculpture of a cormorant by Ewan Berry has been artfully positioned next to a silvery moon globe by Andrew O'Doherty. Around it, a series of gently mounded beds are filled with a dancing froth of ferns, grasses, agapanthus, tulbaghia, and *Euphorbia palustris*, designed to suggest the sea foam and crashing waves of the Atlantic.

The Pond Garden lies nearby, providing a wonderful range of habitats for wildlife. Water-loving plants thrive here, including native species (bog bean, purple loosestrife, *Osmunda regalis*), hostas, water irises, and arum lilies. Next to it sits the Wet Meadow, with its living sculpture of wild rushes. Nearby, the sunny Wildflower Meadow comes alive in early summer with the emergence of many different species, including wild orchids, eyebright, yellow rattle, and hawkweed.

Clockwise from right
The Bird Garden, with sculptures by Ewan Berry and Andrew O'Doherty.

The Exotic Garden, home to handsome tree ferns and ornamental grasses.

The Pond Garden is a haven for wildlife and aquatic plants.

A view across the Walled Kitchen Garden towards Glenveagh Castle and its Victorian Orangery.

Glenveagh Castle Gardens

WHERE *Glenveagh National Park, Church Hill, County Donegal, F92 HR77* WHEN *From late spring when the rhododendrons are in bloom; summer when the gardens are magnificent* WHAT *Historic castle gardens and grounds set within a national park, with a rich horticultural past and important plant collections*

Located in a mountainous valley in the wilds of Donegal, below the craggy peaks of Errigal and Dooish and with views out over the glimmering grey waters of Lough Veagh, Glenveagh Castle and its historic 4.5-hectare (11-acre) gardens have a theatrical, almost surreal quality, underscored by the rugged natural beauty of the surrounding terrain.

Over the last 160 years a succession of great garden makers played an important part in Glenveagh's creation, beginning in 1868 when the castle was built for wealthy land speculator John George Adair. After his death in 1885, the 11,330-hectare (28,000-acre) estate passed to his wife, Cornelia. A gifted plantswoman, she used the site's naturally dramatic topography to stunning effect, creating shelterbelts and laying out the "pleasure grounds" and Belgian Walk.

In 1937, American art collector Henry McIlhenny bought the property, marking the beginning of a golden age for Glenveagh. Advised by noted designers James Russell and Lanning Roper, he greatly expanded the plant collection and developed a series of interlinking gardens.

In 1975, McIlhenny sold the surrounding estate - now Glenveagh National Park - to the Irish State, followed in 1983 by the generous gift of the castle and its gardens. Today, all three are managed by the National Parks and Wildlife Services (NPWS), with the historic gardens under the care of head gardener Seán Ó Gaoithin.

Significant historic elements of their design include the formal Tuscan Garden, with its stone benches, marble busts, and clipped hedges, and the Italian Terrace, with its classical statues and terracotta urns. Other areas of note are the Swiss Walk, View Garden, Himalayan Garden, Glenveagh's famously precipitous "67 Steps", and its stunning Walled Kitchen Garden.

HISTORIC COLLECTIONS

Glenveagh's vast and historically unique plant collection now stretches to 1,700 taxa. It includes 241 varieties of *Rhododendron*, as well as many species of *Magnolia*, *Michelia*, *Eucryphia*, *Styrax*, *Pieris*, *Nothofagus*, and *Gaultheria*, plus collections of heritage varieties of apple, narcissus, and snowdrops. In summer, look out for the garden's famous scarlet-flowered *Dahlia* 'Matt Armour' in the Kitchen Garden.

Kylemore Abbey

WHERE *Kylemore, Connemara, County Galway, H91 VR90* WHEN *Open all year, but displays in the parterre garden and vegetable garden peak in midsummer* WHAT *A restored Victorian walled garden showcasing plants and planting styles dating from pre-1900*

Kylemore Abbey's 2.6-hectare (6½-acre) Walled Garden – a showpiece of Victorian horticulture, now restored by Benedictine nuns – is testament to the vision and resources of eye surgeon and politician Mitchell Henry, who carved it out of a boggy, windswept mountainside.

The approach to Kylemore Abbey's Walled Garden, one of Ireland's largest, is along a former carriageway sheltered by towering Monterey pines and dense woods, which extend around the garden. It beggars belief that when Mitchell Henry bought Kylemore Lodge and its 6,070-hectare (15,000-acre) estate in 1867 this was a marshy wilderness, with just a few remnants of old woodland.

A GARDEN OF TWO HALVES

The brick and stone walls enclose a sloping garden in two parts. Closest to the entrance gate is the parterre, where perennial and annual bedding plants are neatly grown around exotics such as cordylines and phoenix palms in a series of crescent-shaped and circular beds cut out of velvet-green lawns. These create blazes of colour from spring to autumn when sedums, anaphalis, asters, and persicarias extend the season, thanks to the temperate climate. At the top of the slope are the two restored glasshouses to have survived out of the 21 original, one filled with heritage varieties of ornamentals and vegetables, the other a vinery.

The garden is bisected by a stream bordered by woodland planting, which provided a sense of wilderness for the Victorians and is today colonized by banks of orange crocosmia. Beyond this, the space is broken up into a rock garden, a kitchen and herb garden filled with heritage varieties interplanted with vibrant pot marigolds, and a double herbaceous border planted in tiers, creating an orderly arrangement of perennials and annuals.

A GREEN FUTURE

In many ways, stepping into Kylemore's Walled Garden is a journey back to the late 1890s. When the £1.5 million restoration was undertaken in 1995, the team of gardeners worked to a late-Victorian planting plan, and the Benedictine nuns now steer Kylemore as a public garden and place of education, spirituality, and tranquillity. With biodiversity a key element in the estate's sustainability plan, the Victorian reliance on chemicals has been swapped for natural techniques, such as seaweed mulch, organic pest deterrents, and home-made compost.

Above *In the kitchen garden strong-smelling* Tagetes tenuifolia *and* Calendula officinalis *are paired with heritage cabbage 'Red Drumhead' to repel insect pests.*

Right *Blue* Echinops sphaerocephalus *and white* Chrysanthemum superbum *create height in the tiered herbaceous border, with crocosmias adding fiery shades.*

TIMELINE OF EVENTS

1867

Mitchell Henry purchases the Kylemore estate for his wife, Margaret.

1871

His Gothic-style castellated house, overlooking the dark waters of Pollacappul Lough, is completed. During this time, the Walled Garden, complete with 21 glasshouses, is laid out.

1902

After the death of his wife and one of his daughters, Henry sells the estate to the Duke of Manchester and returns to England.

1920

The neglected estate, now 4,047 hectares (10,000 acres) in extent, is sold to a community of Benedictine nuns from battle-torn Ypres in France. They establish a boarding school for girls.

1995

Restoration of the overgrown Walled Garden begins.

A view across the gardens towards the river and handsome stone arches of Caher Bridge.

Caher Bridge Garden

WHERE *Formoyle West, Craggagh, Ballyvaughan, County Clare, H91 H66C*
WHEN *From late spring to autumn* WHAT *A 0.8-hectare (2-acre) contemporary garden by the banks of a river, wonderfully at one with the surrounding wild landscape*

Garden makers who ignore the natural topography of their site do so at their peril; there's always a risk the garden will look and feel a little ill at ease. On the other hand, there are gardens such as Caher Bridge, whose close kinship with the raw-boned landscape of the Burren gives it a sense of what garden designer Russell Page described as "inevitability".

Everywhere throughout this garden, serving as a constant theme and counterbalance to the generous, naturalistic planting, is stone. Dug out of the ground, it's been used to make the low, curling walls that Caher Bridge's owner and creator Carl Wright crafted to contain the precious loads of imported topsoil, as well as in the lofty bridge that spans the nearby Caher River. An important view from the garden, the bridge's arches are deliberately echoed throughout the garden's design to create a pleasing sense of rhythm.

Stone also features in the paths, the new Burren Rock Border of dainty alpines, and the sculptural Moon Window, as well as the new hilltop Folly, which overlooks the Caher Valley. Unsurprisingly, given the location, stone also lies just beneath visitors' feet, the garden's limestone bedrock so close to the surface that it has dictated the positioning of beds and paths.

ELEMENTAL DESIGN

Part of Wright's genius as a garden maker is that he celebrates this elemental quality just as he does Caher Bridge's setting close by the water's edge. Plants that thrive in its damp, cool soil and shady aspect include species of hosta, rodgersia, mahonia, zantedeschia, weigela, iris, brunnera, crataegus, astilbe, and hemerocallis, including many cultivars of Irish origin.

Part of the garden's unique charm also lies in its celebration of the local flora, its wild willow, hazel, hawthorn, and blackthorn, its lacy ferns and the tiny orchids, cowslips, and violets that stud the Wildflower Meadow in early summer. These are preceded by successive displays of bulbous species such as snowdrops, narcissus (the garden has a collection of more than 200 Irish cultivars), and camassia, carefully chosen to look entirely at home. Wildlife also flourishes in the garden, from dragonflies and cuckoos to chiffchaffs and field voles.

A truly biodiverse space, Caher Bridge has been skilfully planted to be ecologically at one with the wild Irish landscape. For the same reason, bright colour has been kept to a minimum – the focus instead is on the subtle interplay between shades and tones of green. An essay in restraint, it proves that less is almost always more.

RHSI Bellefield House & Gardens

WHERE *Shinrone, County Offaly, R42 NW82* WHEN *February during Ireland's annual Snowdrop Month celebration; summer when the flower borders are at their best*
WHAT *Home to a host of botanical treasures in 11.3 hectares (28 acres) of gardens, woodlands, parkland, pasture, and bogland*

Landscape architect, plantsperson, and garden historian Angela Jupe was a dynamic figure in Irish gardening up until her death in 2021. Even now, her influence continues with the bequest of Bellefield, her home and garden, to the Royal Horticultural Society of Ireland.

Jupe was a plant enthusiast and inveterate collector to her core, renowned for her lushly romantic, intricately layered, country-house style of gardening. Particular passions included heritage varieties of roses, bearded irises, clematis, narcissus, tulips, peonies, hellebores, and snowdrops. At the time of her death, she was deep in research for a book she planned to write on Irish varieties of the latter. A noted galanthophile, Jupe played a key role in popularizing this genus of dainty late-winter flowers in Ireland, as well as amassing her own unique collection of more than 200 varieties.

EXPERT GARDEN-MAKING

Jupe also had a magpie's eye combined with an innate sense of style when it came to the business of garden-making, ingeniously repurposing elements of architectural salvage throughout Bellefield's Walled Garden to create handsome garden structures. These include its distinctive folly, "Victorian" glasshouse, and trickling 33-metre- (108ft-) long water rill edged with antique limestone paving. Such were her talents as a garden maker (she trained under designer John Brookes, see page 96) that it's hard to imagine that when she purchased the property back in 2003, the house was semi-derelict and its 3-hectare (7-acre) gardens so overgrown that a sharp slash hook was required to get through them.

Despite Bellefield's free-draining alkaline soil, Jupe also succeeded in creating a charming woodland garden to the front of the handsome early-nineteenth-century house, beneath the dappled shade of the garden's ancient beech trees. Snowdrops thrive in this area in particular, with sheets of the native species *Galanthus nivalis* appearing in early spring.

Appointed as head gardener by the RHSI in 2023, horticulturist Paul Smyth now heads up the sympathetic conservation and development of Bellefield's gardens while ensuring its unique plant collection is carefully catalogued.

FOCUS ON

Species Tulips

Jupe went to great lengths to encourage species-type tulips – including the candy-striped *Tulipa clusiana* 'Lady Jane', gold-and red *T. clusiana* var. *chrysantha*, yellow-flowering *T. batalinii*, scarlet *T. sprengeri*, and ruby-red *T. linifolia* – to naturalize in Bellefield's Walled Garden by deliberately leaving areas of the lawns uncut until at least late July.

Clockwise from top left
Naturalized clumps of Narcissus *blooming in the front lawns.*

Tulipa clusiana *var.* chrysantha *is one of many species tulips planted by Angela Jupe.*

Snowdrops and other spring-flowering bulbs carpet the ground.

Dense ornamental borders include Dahlia *'Bright Eyes',* Linaria *'Peachy', and* Pseudopanax lessonii *'Tuatara'.*

Hunting Brook Gardens

WHERE *Lamb Hill, Blessington, County Wicklow, W91 YK33* WHEN *From early spring, when its extensive snowdrop collection comes into flower, until late autumn* WHAT *A constantly evolving, contemporary 8-hectare (20-acre) country garden created by a passionate plantsperson*

Exuberant, idiosyncratic, exciting, experimental – all are words that have been used to describe the gardens of Hunting Brook in West Wicklow, the creation of gardener, teacher, and author Jimi Blake.

Situated just over 300 metres (984ft) above sea level on the cool, damp, steep, south-facing slopes of Lamb Hill, Hunting Brook is home to explosively colourful flower borders, wildflower meadows, tranquil leafy groves, twisting woodland paths edged with shade-loving treasures, and a plunging Ice Age glen, through which a babbling stream runs.

Jimi Blake's intense love of plants – which he shares in common with his older sister June Blake, whose own remarkable garden lies just a few fields away (see page 220) – first emerged when he was a young child, and was nurtured by his mother, Kathleen. Hunting Brook is a reflection of that lifelong fascination, as well as his enduring readiness to push the boundaries of gardening conventions, be that in terms of plant hardiness or perceived "good taste". As a result, the planting at Hunting Brook is forever evolving as Blake experiments with fresh combinations of new varieties sought out from specialist nurseries and plant fairs, or brought home from his tours of the great gardens of Europe.

THEATRICAL PLANTING

In Hunting Brook's early years, Blake focused on the giant sloping, sunny beds immediately around his home – a log cabin whose tarry-black walls bring to mind Derek Jarman's Garden at Dungeness (see page 82). Redesigned and enlarged in recent years, these flowerbeds are punctuated by tall, handsome specimens of the shrubby tree *Aralia echinocaulis*. Grown from seed that Blake brought home from a plant-hunting expedition in central China, their leafy crowns have been artfully lifted to enhance their sculptural silhouettes.

The planting here first comes to life in spring with a glorious display of narcissus, primula,

Left *The pink bottlebrush flowers of* Sanguisorba menziesii *light up a sunny border in early summer.*

Right *Opium poppies and spires of* Lupin *'Tequila Flame'*[PBR] *bloom beneath multiple specimens of* Aralia echinocaulis.

and pulmonaria, but summer is playtime for Blake, a master propagator who loves to experiment with mass plantings. Hunting Brook is particularly known for its dramatic displays of choice perennials, including single-flowered dahlias raised from seed, often combined with tender exotics and half-hardy species overwintered undercover. A constantly edited community of hardy perennials, trees, and shrubs forms the backbone planting, chosen by Blake for qualities such as a long season of interest, exceptional floriferousness, and vigour.

A CONTEMPORARY WOODLAND

The exuberance of the planting around the house is counterbalanced by Hunting Brook's tranquil woodland gardens, an area of growing fascination for Blake as the gardens mature. Rough pathways edged with foraged timber bring visitors through shady groves filled with handsome specimens of pseudopanax, schefflera, neopanax, bamboo underplanted with swathes of snowdrops (a considerable collection, including many rare varieties), trillium, corydalis, epimedium, podophyllum, and other choice woodlanders.

Over the years Blake has carefully edited the existing larch, sycamore, and spruce woodland to allow for new pathways and generous plantings, while allowing shafts of sunlight to filter in. Many of its new specimens, such as *Heptapleurum taiwanianum*, *Rhododendron sinogrande*, and *Neopanax laetus*, are still in the first flush of youth, but already their presence is transformative.

GARDEN INSPIRATION

Exotic Structure

Shrubby, evergreen members of the *Araliaceae* family add an architectural, exotic air to the planting at Hunting Brook. Borderline-hardy, shade-tolerant species of pseudopanax, tetrapanax, schefflera, heptapleurum, and neopanax are also increasingly being used by modern garden designers as great choices for a tropical or jungle-style city garden.

The mixed woodland of sycamore and larch is continually being edited and developed.

Ornamental perennials combine in dense, intricate layers in the flowerbeds, featuring allium, astrantia, eryngium, and echinacea.

June Blake's Garden

WHERE *Tinode, Blessington, County Wicklow* WHEN *From late spring, when the Robinsonian-style meadow first comes to life, through to late autumn* WHAT *A contemporary Irish country garden and specialist nursery that combines painterly planting with artful design*

Situated in the rugged foothills of the West Wicklow mountains, in an area known for its cool temperatures, high rainfall, and acidic soil, June Blake's Garden is the result of its creator's exacting eye and great talents as a gardener and designer.

Realized over a period of several decades by June Blake, this garden is an outstanding example of how the sensitive renovation of a historic property can be successfully married to contemporary design in ways that enrich both.

The sloping 1.2-hectare (3-acre) site, which wraps itself around a handsome Victorian farm-steward's house and its granite farmyard buildings, enjoys far-off views of the densely wooded, mountainous landscape of West Wicklow. Arranged within a geometric grid of pebbled paths and dry-stone retaining walls, the formality of the garden's giant rectangular flowerbeds and shallow reflective pool is offset by lush, intensely colourful, and intricately layered perennial and woody planting.

From spring to late autumn, that planting performs like a series of acts in a play, each one dramatically beautiful. In spring it's the turn of sheets of hellebores, primulas, tulips, silver-leaved brunnera, pulmonaria, and blue Himalayan poppies. Late-summer stalwarts include tall, single-flowered dahlias, scarlet-flowered monarda, crocosmia, hardy geraniums, rudbeckia, scented phlox, and alstroemeria.

SOFTENING THE EDGES

Above the house and its formal grid of flower beds, a Robinsonian-style (see page 90) sculpted meadow blurs the edges of the garden and connects it to the wilder landscape. Higher up the sloping site, glimpses of historic Tinode House (once owned by the Blake family) are still visible through a clipped hornbeam hedge. In spring, the meadow is studded with scarlet-flowered *Tulipa* 'Red Shine' and baby-blue camassias, followed by native orchids and yellow rattle. Woodland-edge planting around the garden's upper flanks, including specimens of *Cornus kousa*, *Magnolia campbellii*, acers, species rhododendrons, and *Hydrangea aspera* 'Villosa Group', further softens the boundaries.

The site's rich history has been sensitively preserved. Remnants of a centuries-old road, cobbled paths, and dry-stone walls reveal themselves alongside contemporary elements, including the garden's rusted, steel-edged raised beds, meditative garden room, sculptural landforms, topiary larch, and cloud-pruned box tree. Similarly, its specialist nursery is a treasure trove of modern introductions and classics.

The River Valley Garden, with soft layers of woodland planting framing the banks of the Little Dargle River.

Danesmoate Gardens

WHERE *Kellystown Road, Rathfarnham, Dublin, D16 H5P2* WHEN *Year-round interest; best from mid-spring to early autumn* WHAT *A magnificent, privately owned Dublin garden formed around a wooded river valley and home to native wildflower meadows, pools, flower gardens, and a historic walled garden*

A love of gardening is not something generally associated with rock stars, but then the garden of Danesmoate, the Dublin home of Adam Clayton, bass guitarist with the Irish band U2, is no ordinary garden.

Danesmoate's surrounding landscape was predominantly rural when Clayton bought the property back in 1988. Now, the city licks at its boundaries, underscoring the sense of abruptly stepping into a very different world when you pass through its gates.

Dr Neil Murray, the late expert forester and garden designer, advised Clayton on using trees and shrubs to screen the large Georgian house and cocoon it from noise. He also sparked Clayton's passion for magnolias, which now flourish at Danesmoate, including *Magnolia campbellii* 'Darjeeling' and *M.* 'Caerhays Belle'.

RIVERSIDE BEAUTY

The beating heart of the gardens is a plunging, shady river valley, through which the chattering Little Dargle River flows, its course ingeniously manipulated by a series of tumbling waterfalls and quiet weirs built by craftsman Joe Mulligan. A magical place accessed by mossy stone paths and punctuated by multiple bridges, it's half-hidden beneath steep woodland layers of giant beech, yew, sycamore, tree magnolias, and acers underplanted with a lower, leafy storey of smaller magnolias, camellias, rhododendrons, bamboo, hydrangeas, myrtle, holly, iris, and ferns. Fed by trickling mountain springs, the plants' startling growth rate is a matter of pride and wonder for Danesmoate's owner as well as head gardener Darragh Stone and garden advisor Jane Powers.

Recent additions include a contemporary flower garden designed by Wicklow gardener and nursery owner June Blake (see page 220), while the charming historic Walled Garden is home to a new orangerie. A series of small, formal garden rooms sit close by, including the Hot Garden – an intimate space filled with varieties of dahlia, alstroemeria, and tritonia – and the Cold Garden, a secret, shady area defined by clipped yew hedges encircling a fountain. Nearby is a double herbaceous border planted in soft pastel shades. In the native Wildflower Meadow, two naturalistic garden ponds have been created – valuable wildlife-rich habitat in what is a remarkable Irish garden imbued with a unique sense of place.

Airfield Gardens

WHERE *Dundrum, Dublin, D14 EE77* WHEN *Open all year; at its best in midsummer*
WHAT *A 15-hectare (38-acre) urban estate that's run as an educational charity, with a working farm, productive and ornamental gardens, a wildlife pond, and forest walk*

The gardens and model farm at Airfield in the Dublin suburb of Dundrum owe their existence to two remarkable sisters, Laetitia and Naomi Overend, for whom Airfield was home until they handed it over in trust to the people of Ireland in 1974.

The Walled Garden attached to the Overend family's house, where the sisters grew up, was both a productive space, where fruit trees and vegetables were grown, and an ornamental garden. Beyond it were the fields where the philanthropist sisters reared their prize-winning Jersey cows. Today, the same elements can be enjoyed by visitors to Airfield, where the whole estate is run on organic principles, and the produce from the Food Garden supplies the on-site Overends Kitchen.

FUSION PLANTING

One of the drivers of the charity that runs the estate is to inspire visitors to grow their own food. In the Sunken Garden, edible plants such as rosemary, cardoons, lemon verbena, and Chilean guava mingle beautifully with ornamentals such as cannas, bananas, and salvias, which thrive in the shelter of a wavy hornbeam hedge. In the adjoining Walled Garden, the same fusion of edible and ornamental is celebrated, with the original espalier pear trees covering the walls and new espalier crab apples providing vertical structure. A low yew hedge frames a central pergola draped with wisteria, and small borders filled with flowering plants line the paths. Dublin's temperate climate allows tender species such as *Echium* and *Tetrapanax* to flourish in the deep border outside the walls.

A short walk past the restored glasshouse of succulents and cacti leads to the Food Garden, Airfield's beating heart. Gravel paths wind round the beds, which vary from elliptical (with cutting flowers), to rectangular (with vegetables in neat rows), to L-shaped (with bush fruit in cages).

Crops are labelled to show visitors the range they could grow at home, while a line of hazel bushes epitomizes the ethos of these biodiverse and sustainable gardens: the cobnuts are sold at the farmers' market, and the cut stems are used for edging in the estate's community garden.

GARDEN INSPIRATION

Practical Flowers

Edible flowers such as calendula, borage, violas, and nasturtiums are grown for use in Airfield's restaurant, but they also play an important role in attracting pollinators to the Food Garden. Black-eyed Susans are planted in the brassica beds to attract hoverflies and parasitic wasps, and green manures, such as blue-flowered phacelia, purple-flowered summer vetch, and cereal rye, are sown to cover bare soil and suppress weeds.

Top *Rows of lavender in the organic vegetable garden help to attract pollinators.*

Bottom *Structural fruit trees and herbaceous borders combine to frame a feature pergola in the Walled Garden.*

Top *Dating from 1869 and made of zinc, the Pegasus statues rear up sentinel-like beside the Triton Lake.*

Bottom *The sweeping view across Triton Lake towards the series of formal terraces beneath Powerscourt House.*

Powerscourt Gardens

WHERE *Enniskerry, County Wicklow, A98 W0D0* WHEN *Impressive at all times of the year* WHAT *Home to 19 hectares (47 acres) of ornamental gardens, including extensive Italianate formal gardens surrounded by wooded parklands*

Few Irish gardens can compete with the historic demesne of Powerscourt for its spectacular setting, its dramatic layout of staggered, semi-circular formal terraces, and its otherworldly views of the surrounding Wicklow mountains and wooded valleys.

A substantial part of the design at Powerscourt is the work of the famously irascible and intemperate landscape architect Daniel Robertson. Executed over a period of 40 years, it was completed in 1880 by Mervyn Edward Wingfield, 7th Viscount Powerscourt, with the help of his gardener, Alexander Robertson.

At its centre sits the garden's central "perron" – a viewing platform offering uninterrupted views of its sunken parterres, magnificent Triton Lake, and fountain. These are reached by a cascade of stone steps linking the descending terraces and forming the main axis of the design. Other noted elements include the collection of statuary, particularly the glorious twin statues of the mythological winged horse Pegasus.

GARDEN TREASURES

From its central perron or platform, look right to the Walled Garden, home to a lushly colourful double herbaceous border, perfumed rose garden, and Powerscourt's famously beautiful trompe-l'oeil Bamberg Gates.

Off in the distance lies Powerscourt's small Japanese Garden and its decorative Pepperpot Tower, added by the 8th Viscount Powerscourt in the early twentieth century. The celebrated Powerscourt Waterfall (Ireland's highest), lies just 3km (2 miles) south of the gardens, at a height of 121 metres (397ft).

A noted connoisseur and collector of beautiful objets d'art, the 7th Viscount Powerscourt was also a collector of trees. Between 1870 and 1880, he is reputed to have planted four million within the estate. "Nobody", he wrote, "can say that I have not left my mark on the country." That remarkable legacy includes the garden's famous avenue of *Araucaria araucana* – monkey puzzle trees.

In 1961 Mervyn Patrick Wingfield, 9th Viscount Powerscourt, sold the house and gardens to the late Ralph and Gwen Slazenger, ending a continuous line of ownership by the Wingfield family that began in 1609. Tragically, Powerscourt House itself was subsequently badly damaged by fire in 1974 before being substantially rebuilt. But the remarkable gardens endured and are now under the care of head gardener Alexander Slazenger. Now a major tourist attraction, recent biodiversity initiatives include the wildflower meadows, tree-planting programme, and bee sanctuary.

Killruddery House & Gardens

WHERE *Southern Cross, Bray, County Wicklow* WHEN *April to October; particularly beautiful in late spring when its woodland planting is in full bloom* WHAT *A historic Irish country house demesne and working farm with 35 hectares (86½ acres) of ornamental gardens*

Considered one of the finest surviving examples of seventeenth-century garden landscape design in both Ireland and Britain, Killruddery encompasses layers of history. Its French Baroque framework and nineteenth-century additions now play host to a sustainable biodiverse farm and vibrant visitor attraction.

Home to the Brabazon family for more than 400 years, Killruddery House's ornamental gardens and woodlands can be traced back to the late 1600s and the French Baroque style of the time, as exemplified by Versaille landscape architect André Le Nôtre (see opposite).

Many distinctive elements of that original formal design remain extant. They include Killruddery's famous twin Long Ponds, the Beech Circle, the Lime Avenue, the Sylvan Theatre, and the distinctive Angles or *"pattes d'oie"* – angled walks enclosed by high beech, yew, lime, and hornbeam hedges. Later additions include the Lower Parterre, the Walled Kitchen Garden (in its Victorian form), and its Pithouse.

MOVING WITH THE TIMES

Historic gardens of this scale can sometimes rest on their laurels, but not Killruddery. Large-scale renovation and development work carried out by the Brabazon family in recent years, with additional support from heritage funding, has ushered in a new and exciting era.

Restoration of its organically managed Walled Garden and Victorian glasshouse was completed several years ago, its kitchen garden supplying the busy farm shop as well as the estate's award-winning Grain Store restaurant. The Walled Garden's informal air, giant sandpit, colourful cut-flower borders, and resident chickens make this a popular spot for families.

Elsewhere, the parterre offers views out across the rolling lawns and woodlands. Equally charming are the garden's extensive, meandering woodland walks through mature plantings of ornamental shrubs and specimen trees. Managed to support biodiversity, these areas are intentionally gardened with a light hand. For a more challenging walk, make the trek to the Rock, which lies east and uphill of Killruddery House, beyond its formal terraced lawns. Surrounded by shady woodland planting of azaleas, magnolias, rhododendrons, and bulbous species (at their floriferous best in late spring), this elevated spot offers panoramic views of the house and gardens, as well as the surrounding Wicklow Mountains.

Top *The Long Ponds stretch away from the south terrace at the front of the house.*

Bottom *The Lower Parterre or Sunken Garden was laid out in 1869 by Daniel Robertson (see page 226).*

FOCUS ON

French Baroque

The large-scale, imposing grandeur and formality of the French Baroque style is epitomized by the hugely influential gardens of Versailles just outside Paris, on which work began in 1661. Designed by André Le Nôtre for the Sun King Louis XIV, using an infinite-perspective axis from which a series of secondary avenues and pathways radiate, Versailles features intricately elaborate box parterres and yew topiary, shady groves or *"bosquets"*, canals, pools, fountains, and marble statuary.

Autumn colour along the River Vartry, which flows down numerous weirs in its progress through the gardens.

Mount Usher Gardens

WHERE *Ashford, County Wicklow, A67 VW22* WHEN *Mid- to late spring when the woodlands and meadows are at their peak; autumn for its seasonal foliage displays* WHAT *A world-famous, organically managed woodland garden located in East Wicklow*

The gardens at Mount Usher exemplify what's known as the Robinsonian style, a romantically informal, naturalistic approach to garden-making championed by the hugely influential Irish gardener, publisher, and author William Robinson.

Located in a sheltered valley that enjoys a very protected microclimate where tender species thrive, Mount Usher combines a majestic woodland garden with exuberant flower borders, but is also very much a water garden. Its topography and layout are defined by the River Vartry and its tributary, the River Killiskey, which both run through the heart of its densely planted acres along with the remains of an old millrace. The result is an exceptionally charming and biodiverse space that's very rich in wildlife.

AN ERICACEOUS COLLECTION

Home to more than 4,500 species of plants, Mount Usher is known for its outstanding collection of ericaceous trees and shrubs, which includes many species of rhododendron, azalea, eucalyptus, magnolia, daphne, nothofagus, davidia, cornus, acer, eucryphia, hoheria, and crinodendron. There are also choice conifers to be found, such as *Agathis australis* (New Zealand kauri pine), *Pinus montezumae* (Mexican blue pine), *Juniperus recurva* var. *coxii* (coffin juniper), *Picea breweriana* (Brewer's weeping spruce), and more than 20 champion trees (see page 93). An extended "tree walk" guides visitors around the woodlands, with each specimen numbered and named in the accompanying leaflet.

Large drifts of naturalized bulbous perennials, including snowdrops, scilla, narcissi, erythronium, anemones, bluebells, and wild garlic, carpet the woodland meadows in spring, followed in early summer by clouds of wild orchids and sprinkles of *Lilium martagon* and *Lilium pyrenaicum*. Along the river's damp, shallow banks, moisture-loving perennials thrive, including species of primula, rheum, and darmera.

THROUGH THE GENERATIONS

Almost 160 years in the making, the story of this 9-hectare (22-acre) country garden begins in 1868 when the wealthy Dublin linen merchant Edward Walpole purchased the property, then an old tuck mill located on 0.4 hectares (1 acre) of land. Edward began to develop the gardens, before gifting Mount Usher to his three sons, George, Edward, and Thomas Walpole, in 1875. Passionate plantspeople and early devotees of William Robinson (see page 90; Robinson wrote

Clockwise from top

Bluebells carpet the ground in the Eucalyptus Grove, as Pyrenean lilies start to show.

Streamside planting in the Island area includes hostas and candelabra primulas.

Beech hedging protects the double herbaceous borders, at their best in summer.

of his admiration for Mount Usher in his book *The English Flower Garden*, published in 1889), George and Edward continued to develop the gardens in the naturalistic Robinsonian style. They were helped by the fact that they were friends with many influential gardeners of their era, including Sir Frederick Moore of Ireland's National Botanic Gardens, botanist Augustine Henry, F.W. Burbidge of Trinity College Botanic Garden, and horticulturalist E.A. Bowles, who sent botanical treasures their way.

The Walpoles sourced many other rare plants for the greatly extended gardens from specialist nurseries in Europe, Australia, and Japan. The engineering-minded Thomas was also responsible for creating Mount Usher's series of bridges, small streams, and weirs, the latter crucial for preserving water levels in summer. The brothers were eventually succeeded by Edward Jr's son, the distinguished gardener and brilliant plantsperson E. Horace Walpole, who continued the family's expert stewardship and enhancement of the gardens. He, in turn, was succeeded by his son, Robert.

ENDURING BEAUTY

In 1980, the Walpole family sold Mount Usher to the late Madelaine Jay, who fell in love with the garden and instigated its sensitive, skilful rejuvenation under the expert care of its then head gardener, John Anderson (now keeper of the gardens of the Windsor Estate in England and recipient of the RHS Veitch Medal). Madelaine's number-one rule was that the garden would be entirely organic, with no chemicals used.

In 2007, the gardens were leased out to the Avoca Handweavers chain, which subsequently established a thriving restaurant and gift shop within the grounds. With the support of Madelaine Jay's son, Konrad, and Avoca, this unique garden continues to thrive under the expert care of head gardener Sean Heffernan.

GARDEN INSPIRATION

Ericaceous Planting

The term "ericaceous" refers to species of lime-hating plants that require an acidic soil where the pH is ideally between 5.1 and 6.0. The pH of any garden's soil is typically defined by the underlying type of bedrock and can be easily measured using a home testing kit. In gardens with alkaline soils where the pH is above 7, it's possible to artificially create a raised bed suitable for selected ericaceous plants by filling it with imported acidic soil or ericaceous compost.

FOCUS ON

Kilmacurragh's Rhododendrons

The unique collection of rhododendrons at Kilmacurragh includes over 180 species and more than 420 named varieties. These shrubby, ericaceous plants come to a floriferous peak in the gardens in early April, their beauty celebrated with guided tours of the garden, lectures, and video stories as part of Kilmacurragh's annual Rhododendron Week.

Above *The double herbaceous border, rich with echium, knautia, salvia, and catmint.*

Right *Kilmacurragh's famous Broad Walk of yews and rhododendrons in brilliant pink bloom.*

National Botanic Gardens, Kilmacurragh

WHERE *Kilmacurragh, Kilbride, County Wicklow, A67 YR12* WHEN *From mid-spring when the woodlands and ornamental rhododendron walks come into bloom*
WHAT *A historic estate famed for its woodlands and ericaceous plants*

In the world of Irish gardens, Kilmacurragh is a prize jewel, a place steeped in the history of famous plant hunters, great garden makers, and exceptional plantspeople, yet which somehow also succeeds in being very modern.

The sister garden of Ireland's National Botanic Gardens, Glasnevin, this historic 42-hectare (104-acre) East Wicklow estate is famed for its outstanding collection of unusual Southern Hemisphere conifers, rhododendrons, and other ericaceous species that flourish in its mild, damp microclimate and deep acidic soil.

From the late 1600s until the early 1900s, Kilmacurragh was home to the Acton family, who left their mark upon it in myriad ways, from its centuries-old lime avenue to its Regency Walled Garden and Rhododendron Walks.

Most significant were siblings Janet and Thomas Acton, who lived at Kilmacurragh between 1824 and 1908. Their love of plants, and exceptional skills as garden makers led to the gardens being stocked with a wealth of exciting new species collected by some of the greatest plant hunters of the day.

That treasure trove of plants includes the remarkable Broad Walk of Irish yews and rhododendrons, planted by Janet Acton as a formal avenue in 1874 – now graceful giants whose canopies intertwine overhead. By mid-spring, this area is filled with the huge scarlet flower clusters of the Highclere rhododendron, *R.* 'Altaclarense'.

REBIRTH

The twentieth century was not kind to Kilmacurragh, and by the time the Office of Public Works took it over in 1996, the house was a roofless ruin. But under the inspired stewardship of head gardener Seamus O'Brien, it has enjoyed a dramatic reversal of fortunes, including the restoration of its species-rich hay meadows and the development of its Walled Garden and extended woodlands. O'Brien has also added thousands of new plants, including many raised from seed collected on his plant-hunting expeditions to China, Chile, and Tasmania. There are also plans in place to restore Kilmacurragh House, one of the final pieces in the puzzle.

The prairie-style planting, woody framework, and borrowed views of the new Torc Garden.

Patthana Gardens

WHERE *Kiltegan, County Wicklow, W91 X789* WHEN *From mid-spring, when the flower borders come to life, until late autumn* WHAT *An artist's country garden, known for its painterly use of colour and its owners' love of nature*

There is a long and distinguished history of artists channelling their talents into the creation of exceptional gardens, from Claude Monet at Giverny to Derek Jarman at Dungeness (see page 82). T.J. Maher is another, with an artist's sensibility that shines brightly at Patthana, the country garden that he's created over the last three decades.

Maher's sensitive use and deep understanding of colour – of its ability to create mood and atmosphere and punctuate a space – particularly stands out at Patthana. Shades of electric pink, fluorescent orange, and saturated violet-purple, repeated in successive waves throughout the growing year, give the planting a luminous quality. In spring, it's the turn of tulips such as 'Dordogne', 'Negrita', 'Ballerina', 'Apricot Impression', and 'Orange Emperor', used in combination with honesty, wallflowers, and geums, plus hyacinths and Dutch irises.

By high summer, these have been replaced with high-performing perennials and a generous smattering of annuals and biennials, with the focus on long-flowering, resilient varieties. Examples include *Linaria* 'Dial Park' and *L.* 'Peachy', *Geranium* 'Rozanne' and *G.* 'Anne Thomson', and *Helenium* 'Sahin's Early Flowerer'.

ROOTED IN THE LANDSCAPE

That exuberant display stands in startling contrast to the muted shades of slate-blue, green, and grey that define the wilder Wicklow landscape surrounding Maher and his husband Simon Kirby's home. Evidence of the property's deep-rooted ties to that rural landscape and its agricultural past are celebrated as part of its historical fabric. These include granite steps leading to the Upper Terrace, made of old saddle stones found on-site. Likewise, the handsome metal pillars supporting the rose-covered pergola were found on-site, as were the moss-covered granite cobblestones paving its Lower Courtyard.

Located next to the house, Patthana's sheltered courtyards are home to a sunken garden and tiny, tranquil wildlife-friendly pond. In spring and summer, generous huddles of pots give dramatically colourful displays.

In 2020, the purchase of a field adjacent to the house allowed for the creation of the Torc Garden. The focus here is on rich, multilayered planting with a long season of interest. The framework of woody specimens includes stewartia, eucalyptus, paulownia, ailanthus, cornus, and quercus. In the distance is the local church, a borrowed view that adds both charm and a deep sense of place.

Top *Mature beech trees growing in the Nun's Walk.*

Bottom *The Corona North Commemorative Border, with catmint, delphiniums, and geraniums in bloom.*

Altamont Gardens

WHERE *Tullow, County Carlow, R93 N882* WHEN *February for snowdrops; midsummer for herbaceous borders; autumn for fiery foliage* WHAT *One of Ireland's best-loved country gardens, home to an internationally significant collection of snowdrops and extensive woodlands arranged around a large informal manmade lake*

When it comes to charm, atmosphere, and a sense of place, Altamont has all three in barrowloads. That's partly due to its romantic setting in rural Carlow, but also to its late owner, Corona North, who bequeathed the property to the State after her death in 1999.

Named by her father, Feilding Lecky Watson, after his favourite rhododendron, North was an intrepid, indefatigable, and generous-minded gardener whose endless enthusiasm, work ethic, and love of plants is still evident at Altamont. After returning to live on the estate following her father's death in 1943, she dedicated the rest of her life to the herculean task of renovating, maintaining, and extending its 16-hectare (40-acre) ornamental gardens, often working alone, on a shoestring budget.

One of the first challenges she undertook was cleaning out its badly silted-up 1-hectare (2.5-acre) lake. Above it sits Altamont House, linked to the lake by a formal avenue flanked with topiaried Irish yews, box hedging, and roses. To one side is Altamont's famous Nun's Walk, where hellebores and snowdrops grow beneath the shady canopy of old beech trees.

Snowdrops were an enduring passion, one North nurtured among the gardeners and friends who helped her tend Altamont in her later years. These include galanthophile Robert Miller, who runs Altamont Plants, the specialist nursery in the charming Walled Garden, which is also home to the magnificent Corona North Commemorative Border. The nursery is run independently to the gardens and estate, which are managed by the Office of Public Works (OPW). Both are known internationally for their extensive collections of snowdrops, which stretch to almost 600 hundred varieties and attract thousands of visitors during Altamont's annual Snowdrop Month in February.

NATURALISTIC WOODLAND

Around the lake and in the surrounding Bog Garden and woodlands grow ornamental trees and shrubs planted by North and her father, including varieties of rhododendron, dogwood, camellia, pieris, magnolia, acer, and tulip tree. Other specimens are older again, including Irish yews, giant redwoods, and native sessile oaks.

The Woodland Walk skirts around the lake and through the Bog Garden before descending through Altamont's shady Ice Age Glen filled with mossy stone boulders, trickling streams, rhododendrons, and ancient oaks. It then opens to majestic views along the River Slaney. From here, Altamont's famous "100 Steps" lead back to the gardens, offering distant views of the Blackstairs Mountains.

FOCUS ON

Gertrude Jekyll

The influence of the famous British garden designer Gertude Jekyll (1843–1942) can be seen in many gardens to this day. Along with her great skills as a plantsperson, she was known for her impressionistic style of herbaceous border designs. The use of colour was very carefully orchestrated, beginning with hot shades, which then progressively became cooler and paler along the border's length before heating up again.

Top *Tall plumes of ornamental grasses in bloom in Lismore Castle's Walled Garden.*

Bottom *The ancient Yew Walk in the castle's cool, shady Lower Garden.*

Lismore Castle Gardens

WHERE *Lismore, County Waterford, P51 EY68* WHEN *From March to October; at its best in summer* WHAT *A centuries-old Irish castle garden, home to magnificent flower borders, cut-flower beds, rare ericaceous species, an art gallery, sculpture, and ancient yew walk*

A fairytale huddle of ancient stone walls, turrets, and towers poised high above the banks of the majestic River Blackwater, Lismore Castle appears as if by magic to approaching visitors. Owned by the Devonshire family since 1753, and under the care of head gardener Colm O'Driscoll since 2022, its terraced garden is a beautiful thing of two halves.

In the Upper Garden lies Lismore Castle's early-seventeenth-century Walled Garden. Framed by yew hedges, its double-herbaceous border has been artfully positioned to frame a charming view of St Carthage's Cathedral and incorporates the principles of colour graduation espoused by designer Gertrude Jekyll (see opposite). Nearby are productive beds filled with vegetables, herbs, and fruit, alongside new areas of ornamental planting. The art gallery, established in 2006, looks out over this area.

In a sunny corner by the recently restored Vinery is the new Sand Garden, where heat-loving species including yucca, verbascums, and salvias flourish. Nearby, the cut-flower bed continues a centuries-old tradition of supplying the castle with fresh blooms. The peaceful Sundial Garden was once a sunny spot, but the spreading canopy of mature ornamental cherries (including *Prunus* 'Shirotae') has transformed it into a shady bower. Close by grows the rare Japanese snowbell tree, *Styrax japonicus*.

A very special specimen of *Cryptomeria japonica*, produced from seed given to Deborah, the late Duchess of Devonshire, by her sister Pamela Mitford in the 1950s, can be found at the entrance to the nearby apple orchard. Wild grasses and wildflowers flourish here beneath the fruit trees, a wonderfully effective way to attract pollinators and support biodiversity.

POETIC SPLENDOUR

In the shadier Lower Garden, much of the layout is the work of architect Sir Joseph Paxton (see page 39). Informal in style, this area contains a fine selection of *Camellia* (*C.* 'Saint Ewe'), *Rhododendron* (*R. barbatum*, *R. luteum*, and *R. augustinii*), *Eucryphyia* (*E.* 'Rostrevor'), *Davidia involucrata*, *Nothofagus dombeyi*, and other acid-lovers, as well as an ancient yew walk where Edmund Spenser reputedly wrote part of his epic poem *The Faerie Queene* in 1590.

The rare, evergreen *Magnolia delavayi*, whose fragrant flowers appear intermittently in summer, also grows here. A champion specimen (see page 93), it's believed to be the tallest of its kind in Ireland. Behind the Lily Pond is a pretty fern garden dominated by the magnificent black tree fern *Cyathea medullaris*. Art connoisseurs will also enjoy sculptures by Eilis McConnell and David Nash beautifully positioned among the shady clearings.

Blarney Castle Gardens

WHERE *Blarney, County Cork, T23 Y598* WHEN *From January for snowdrops and narcissus, to autumn for fiery colour* WHAT *A large, exciting Irish garden in the heart of a centuries-old country estate, with historic plantings enhanced and enlarged in recent years*

Dramatically situated on a rocky outcrop with views over the lush Cork countryside, Blarney Castle has long been known for its kissing stone, which legend says gives the "gift of the gab" or eloquence. Now, however, the fifteenth-century castle's gardens are increasingly rivalling the stone as a world-class attraction in their own right.

Working with Blarney's owners, Sir Charles and Lady Caroline Colthurst, gardens manager Adam Whitbourn has revitalized and enhanced this historic 607-hectare (1,500-acre) Irish estate's gardens and arboreta over the last 20 years, combining sensitive conservation and rejuvenation with new areas of interest.

FRESH IDEAS

Among the latter is Blarney's magnificent Fern Garden, a shady place of towering, whiskery tree ferns encircling a trickling water cascade. Other new elements include the double herbaceous border. Measuring 100 metres (328ft) long, its densely planted beds are framed by a handsome pergola clad in creamy-white climbing *Rosa* 'City of York' and coral-pink *Rosa* 'François Juranville', with wisteria at either end.

Elsewhere, the Himalayan Valley is filled with spring-flowering shrubby species, especially rhododendrons, whose large, colourful blooms provide a marvellous display in mid-spring. Most majestic is the garden's multi-stemmed *Rhododendron* 'Cornish Red'. Clusters of luminous scarlet blossoms cover its vast canopy of branches from late February to early May.

The Poison Garden, home to plants such as henbane, mandrake, hemlock, wormwood, and poison ivy, is hugely popular. Some plants are so toxic or rich in narcotic or hallucinogenic properties that they're grown in metal cages to ensure the safety of visitors. Nearby is the garden's Carnivorous Courtyard, where Venus flytrap, voodoo lilies, sundew, and pitcher plants are grown, while other new garden areas include the Seven Sisters and Tropical Border. Blarney Castle is also known for its collection of plant cultivars of Irish origin.

ANCIENT HISTORY

Some of Blarney Castle's more established tree and shrubby plantings were designed by the great nurseryman Sir Harold Hillier (see page 100) in the latter half of the twentieth century. Others are much older, including its azalea-filled Belgian beds, its mature limes, Monterey pine (*Pinus radiata*), and famous Western red cedar (*Thuja plicata*). However, even these can't compete with the castle's ancient yew trees (*Taxus baccata*) in the Rock Close area, which dendrologists estimate to be in the region of 600 years old.

Right *Clumps of golden-flowered rudbeckia light up the sunny borders in the Seven Sisters Garden.*

Far right *Blarney's 100-metre- (328ft-) long herbaceous border, framed by its rose-clad pergola.*

FOCUS ON

Species Conservation

Adam Whitbourn has raised hundreds of young rhododendrons from seed sown under cover in Blarney's glasshouses, which are gradually being added to existing plantings as well as new areas within the gardens. The latter includes the Vietnamese Woodland, an ex-situ conservation project created with the aim of conserving rare, endangered, and possibly even new-to-cultivation species grown from seed collected by Whitbourn in northern Vietnam.

The Italian Garden, with its formal pool and colonnaded Tea House.

Ilnacullin

WHERE *Garinish Island, Bantry, County Cork, P75 X567* WHEN *From late spring to autumn* WHAT *An enchanting subtropical island garden in Bantry Bay*

To reach the magical island garden of Ilnacullin off the coast of West Cork, visitors must take a small ferry boat from the picturesque fishing village of Glengarriff, a short voyage through the peaceful, seal-filled waters of beautiful Bantry Bay to Garinish Island.

When Belfast-born Scottish MP John Annan Bryce and his wife, Violet, bought Garinish back in 1910, it was a rocky, windswept, "goat-ridden" outcrop of 12 hectares (35 acres). To create any sort of garden here must have seemed a fantastical idea, but with the help of gifted British architect Harold Peto (see page 108) and brilliant Scottish horticulturist Murdo MacKenzie, the Bryces made one of mystical beauty.

Peto helped to design the garden's beautiful bone structure that exists to this day; its formal terraces, pool, colonnades, open pavilions, Tea House, Temple, Walled Garden, and stone steps. But it was Murdo Mackenzie who took note of the salt-laden winds, heavy rainfall, and very shallow topsoil, then set about creating ingenious ways to make a sheltered microclimate where tender species could flourish.

NEW BEGINNINGS

In 1953, the Bryce family generously bequeathed Ilnacullin to the Irish State. Now imaginatively managed by the OPW, their island home, Bryce House, has been sensitively renovated, while the gardens are being skilfully rejuvenated under the care of foreman Glyn Sherratt.

Fortunately, much of the woody backbone of the original subtropical planting has survived. This includes ericaceous species such as camellia, embothrium, myrtle, azalea, callistemon, drimys, olearia, ozothamnus, and eucryphia. The gardens are also home to some outstanding rare conifers, including *Dacrydium cupressinum*, *Taiwaniana cryptomerioides*, and *Phyllocladus glaucus*.

In Ilnacullin's Walled Garden, the "laboratory of the gardens", the once-overgrown space is being imaginatively replanted using a mixture of productive and ornamental species. Sensitive editing of other overgrown areas continues.

In the Italian Garden, the planting is being steered back to its original early-twentieth-century style with the use of exotic-looking species, including agave, aeonium, *Myosotidium hortensia*, and *Bergenia ciliata*. Its centuries-old bonsai specimens have also been restored. Impressively, Sherratt manages the gardens in accordance with organic principles. Ilnacullin, it seems, is once again in very safe hands.

Lush, naturalized ferns fringe the edges of the woodland river walks.

Kells Bay

WHERE *Kells, Cahersiveen, County Kerry, V23 EP48* WHEN *Year-round interest; best in early summer* WHAT *A subtropical garden on the southwest coast of Ireland that's home to the largest collection of tree ferns in the Northern Hemisphere, as well as many other exotic species*

Tackling the renovation of a beautiful but dilapidated Victorian hunting lodge and its 10 hectares (25 acres) of unique but overgrown gardens in the wilds of Kerry would be a daunting prospect for most. For its owner, however – the plant explorer, nurseryman, and fern expert Billy Alexander – it has been a labour of love spanning 20 years.

Kells Bay's subtropical gardens were first laid out by the Blennerhassett family in the 1890s, incorporating a walled garden, curved driveway, and extensive woodlands. Plantsman Roy Lancaster also played a key role in the 1980s, introducing many rare shrubs and trees to its then owners, the Vogel family. But by the time Alexander took it on, much of the garden was an impenetrable thicket, its historic plantings compromised by the invasive *Rhododendron ponticum*. Described by Alexander as "a machete job", it took years to restore.

PRIMAEVAL RAINFOREST

Today, the gardens' woodlands are the jewel in its crown. A magical place of shady river walks, tumbling waterfalls, secret pools, bamboo glades, and groves of spectacular tree ferns, it conjures up the sense of an untouched rainforest.

Some of its oldest specimens of *Dicksonia antarctica* – Kells Bay has several thousand – date back to the Victorian era and have reached a stupendous size, their arching fronds reaching up to 4 metres (13ft). In fact, so well does the garden's temperate climate and high annual rainfall suit this species that it long ago became naturalized. Other tree ferns that thrive in Kells Bay's Primaeval Forest include *Dicksonia squarrosa*, *D. fibrosa*, and *Cyathea dealbata*. Beneath them grow many smaller fern species, including blechnum, asplenium, platycerium, and *Todea barbara*, while others grow as epiphytes on the branches of trees, including microsorum and polypodium.

Nearby, a suspended rope bridge adds a fun touch, as do the giant tree-trunk carvings of dinosaurs by artists Pieter Koning and Nathan Solomon. The Cliff Walk offers magnificent views across the landscape to the ancient pilgrim site of Knocknadobar.

In the sheltered terraces of the Ladies Walled Garden grow a wonderful collection of Southern Hemisphere species, including *Pseudopanax crassifolius* from New Zealand, with its strange, leathery, fossil-like leaves.

Ferns grow here, too, including a venerable Victorian *Dicksonia antarctica*, fondly referred to as Kells Bay's "mother tree fern", believed to be the parent plant of its hundreds of mature specimens. From the house, enjoy magnificent views out over mature palm trees, yuccas, and succulents to Kells Bay and Dingle Bay.

Index

RHS Partner Gardens

All RHS members gain free entry to the five RHS gardens with a guest at any time of year. These are: RHS Wisley in Surrey, RHS Bridgewater in Salford, RHS Rosemoor in North Devon, RHS Hyde Hall in Essex, and RHS Harlow Carr near Harrogate. Additionally, RHS Members can visit over 200 Partner Gardens on RHS Member Days, and 41 of these gardens are included in the book. Whether well-known formal landscapes, gardens with contemporary planting designs, wildlife havens, or little-known woodland gems, RHS Partner Gardens support the charitable work of the RHS and offer inspiration to keen gardeners throughout the year.

rhs.org.uk/gardens/partner-gardens/find-a-partner-garden contains information on all the current RHS Partner Gardens in the UK and overseas, and you can find those local to you or places to discover on your travels. Always check the garden's website directly before you set off to confirm free entry dates and times, or any special terms and conditions. Remember to take your RHS Membership card to gain entry; scans or photographs of cards are not accepted. Free RHS Member Days apply to the garden only, and a separate entry fee will be charged to visit associated palaces, houses or attend special events.

Visitor Information

KEY TO SYMBOLS

- ● RHS Garden or Partner Garden
- ⊡ Café and/or restaurant
- ▼ Plant sales
- ☻ Children's play area
- ◪ Dogs allowed (as well as service dogs)
- ◕ Visit by appointment only

ENGLAND / NORTH

The Alnwick Garden ⊡ ▼ ☻

Lowther Castle Gardens ⊡ ▼ ☻ ◪

Levens Hall ⊡ ▼ ☻
Dogs only permitted in specific courtyard areas.

Gresgarth Hall ⊡
Occasional plant stalls from local nurseries.

Newby Hall Gardens ⊡ ▼ ☻

Breezy Knees ⊡ ▼

RHS Garden Harlow Carr ● ⊡ ▼ ☻ ◪ Dogs only permitted at dog walking events.

York Gate ⊡ ▼

Grey to Green, Sheffield ⊡ ◪ Monthly flower market.

Tatton Park ● ⊡ ▼ ☻ ◪

RHS Garden Bridgewater ● ⊡ ▼ ☻

ENGLAND / MIDLANDS

Chatsworth ⊡ ▼ ☻ ◪

Biddulph Grange ● ⊡ ▼ ☻
Dogs only permitted in parkland and picnic areas.

Trentham ⊡ ▼ ☻ ◪

Dorothy Clive Garden ● ⊡ ▼ ☻ ◪

Stockton Bury Gardens ⊡ ▼ ◪

Stone House Cottage Garden & Nursery ▼

Hill Close Gardens ● ⊡ ▼ ☻ ◪
Children's garden for learning and play.

Thenford Arboretum & Gardens ◕ Visits by pre-booked private tour only or on open days, when refreshments are available and there may be plant sales from specialist nurseries.

ENGLAND / EAST

East Ruston Old Vicarage Garden ● ⊡ ▼

The Bressingham Gardens ● ⊡ ▼ ☻

Wrest Park ⊡ ☻ ◪

Beth Chatto Gardens ● ⊡ ▼

RHS Garden Hyde Hall ● ⊡ ▼ ☻

ENGLAND / SOUTH EAST

Broughton Grange ⊡ ▼

Stowe Gardens ● ⊡ ▼ ☻ ◪

Waterperry Gardens ● ⊡ ▼ ☻
Dogs allowed in estate only.

Jellicoe & Aga Khan Gardens ⊡ Aga Khan gardens only by tour; Jellicoe is public space where dogs are allowed.

Claremont Landscape Garden ⊡ ▼ ☻ ◪

RHS Garden Wisley ● ⊡ ▼ ☻

Derek Jarman's Garden ⊡ ◕ Visits to Prospect Cottage itself must be pre-booked.

Great Dixter ⊡ ▼

Sissinghurst Castle Garden ● ⊡ ▼ ☻

Gravetye Manor ⊡ ◕
Visit on pre- booked tours or when dining, or staying at the hotel.

Borde Hill ● ⊡ ▼ ☻ ◪

Sussex Prairies Wild ⊡ ◪ ◕
Open to general public in August, otherwise by pre-booked tour.

Denmans Garden ● ⊡ ▼ ◪

West Dean Gardens ● ⊡ ▼ ☻ ◪

Sir Harold Hillier Gardens ● ⊡ ▼ ☻

Farringford ● ⊡ ◕

ENGLAND / SOUTH WEST

Hidcote ● ⊡ ▼ ◪
Dogs allowed Thurs–Sat, excl. the Old Garden.

Knoll Gardens ● ▼

Iford Manor ⊡ ▼ ◪

Hauser & Wirth ⊡

The Newt in Somerset ● ⊡ ◕ Membership required to visit, or if dining.

Abbotsbury Subtropical Gardens ● ⊡ ▼ ☻ ◪

RHS Garden Rosemoor ● ⊡ ▼ ☻

The Garden House ● ⊡ ▼ ☻

Wildside ▼

The Lost Gardens of Heligan ● ⊡ ▼ ☻ ◪

Trebah ● ⊡ ▼ ☻ ◪

Tremenheere Sculpture Gardens ⊡ ▼ ◪

Trengwainton ⊡ ▼ ◪

Tresco Abbey Garden ⊡ ◪

WALES / NORTH

Plas Cadnant Hidden Gardens

Bodnant Garden

Plas Brondanw

Powis Castle Garden

WALES / SOUTH

Veddw House Garden

Aberglasney

Picton Castle

Dyffryn Fernant

SCOTLAND / HIGHLANDS

Lip na Cloiche

Attadale Gardens

Inverewe

Cawdor Castle

Gordon Castle Walled Garden

Pitmedden Garden

Crathes Castle Garden

SCOTLAND / LOWLANDS

Scone Palace

Backhouse Rossie Estate

Cambo

Shepherd House Garden

Broadwoodside

Floors Castle

Dumfries House

Glenwhan Gardens & Arboretum

Logan Botanic Garden

IRELAND / NORTHERN IRELAND

Mount Stewart House & Gardens

Rowallane Garden

Hillsborough Castle Gardens

IRELAND / REPUBLIC OF IRELAND

Cluain na dTor

Glenveagh Castle Gardens

Kylemore Abbey

Caher Bridge Garden

Visits by pre-booked guided tour.

RHSI Bellefield House & Gardens

Hunting Brook Gardens

June Blake's Gardens

Dogs only allowed if also staying in the accommodation.

Danesmoate Gardens

Visits only as part of a pre-booked group tour.

Airfield Gardens

Powerscourt Gardens

Kilruddery House & Gardens

Mount Usher Gardens

National Botanic Gardens, Kilmacurragh

Patthana Gardens

Altamont Gardens

Lismore Castle Gardens

Blarney Castle Gardens

Ilnacullin

Kells Bay

Acknowledgements

The publisher would like to thank the following for their kind permission to reproduce their photographs:

(Key: a-above; b-below/bottom; c-centre; f-far; l-left; r-right; t-top)

2-3 RHS: Jason Ingram; image shows RHS Garden Bridgewater. **4 RHS:** Jason Ingram; image shows RHS Garden Wisley. **5 Alamy Stock Photo:** The National Trust Photolibrary (l); image shows Powis Castle Garden. **Ray Cox:** (c); image shows Cawdor Castle. **Marianne Majerus Garden Images:** (r); image shows June Blake's Garden. **6 Julie Skelton:** (tl). **6-7 Richard Bloom:** (b). **Marianne Majerus Garden Images:** Marianne Majerus (t). **8 Ray Cox:** (l). **8-9 RHS:** Jason Ingram. **9 Marianne Majerus Garden Images:** Marianne Majerus (r). **12-13 The Alnwick Garden:** Phil Wilkinson. **15 GAP Photos:** Carole Drake (t, b). **16-17 Richard Bloom:** (t). **Joe Wainwright:** (b). **19 Andrew Lawson:** (t, b). **20-21 Ray Cox**. **22-23 Joe Wainwright:** (t). **22 Joe Wainwright:** (b). **23 Joe Wainwright:** (b). **24-25 RHS:** Richard Bloom. **26-27 RHS:** Jason Ingram (t, b). **27 RHS:** Richard Bloom (tr). **29 Richard Bloom:** (t). **GAP Photos:** Carole Drake (b). **30 Richard Bloom:** (t, b). **32-33 Joe Wainwright**. **34-35 RHS:** Neil Holmes (t); Jason Ingram (b). **36-37 RHS:** Jason Ingram. **38 Richard Bloom:** (t). **GAP Photos:** Charles Hawes (b). **40-41 Alamy Stock Photo:** Alex Ramsay. **42-43 Joe Wainwright**. **44-45 GAP Photos:** Fiona Lea. **45 GAP Photos:** Mark Bolton (tl); Dave Zubraski (tr). **46 GAP Photos:** Jenny Lilly (tr). **Joe Wainwright:** (tl, b). **48-49 Marianne Majerus Garden Images**. **50 Jason Ingram:** (t, bl). **50-51 Jason Ingram:** (b). **53 Alamy Stock Photo:** Colin Underhill (tr, b). **GAP Photos:** Rob Whitworth (tl). **54-55 Clive Nichols**. **56-57 Richard Bloom**. **58-59 Richard Bloom**. **60-61 Getty Images:** Heritage Images. **62 Richard Bloom:** (br). **Marianne Majerus Garden Images:** (bl). **62-63 Julie Skelton:** (t). **64-64 RHS:** Richard Bloom. **66 RHS:** Oliver Dixon (t). **66-67 RHS:** Daniel Bridge (b). **67 RHS:** Jason Ingram (t). **68 GAP Photos:** Abigail Rex (t, b). **70-71 Alamy Stock Photo:** Zoonar GmbH. **73 GAP Photos:** Clive Nichols (t, b). **74-75 Alamy Stock Photo:** Hufton & Crow - VIEW (b). **Tom Stuart-Smith Studio:** Jiaji Wu (t). **76 Alamy Stock Photo:** The National Trust Photolibrary / Andrew Butler (t, b). **78-79 RHS:** Jason Ingram. **80-81 Marianne Majerus Garden Images:** Marianne Majerus (t). **80 RHS:** Jason Ingram (bl). **81 RHS:** Joanna Kossak (br). **82 Marianne Majerus Garden Images:** Marianne Majerus (tl, tr). **82-83 Alamy Stock Photo:** Mark Mercer (b). **84-85 Richard Bloom**. **86-87 National Trust Images:** Andrew Butler. **89 National Trust Images:** Andrew Butler (t, b). **90 GAP Photos:** Mark Bolton (t). **90-91 Richard Bloom:** (b). **92-93 Borde Hill Garden:** Claudia Gaupp @ between.gardens (b). **93 Alamy Stock Photo:** Jim Holden (tl). **Marianne Majerus Garden Images:** Marianne Majerus (tr). **94-95 Marianne Majerus Garden Images:** Marianne Majerus. **96-97 Marianne Majerus Garden Images:** Marianne Majerus. **98 Alamy Stock Photo:** Christopher Nicholson (tl). **GAP Photos:** Jacqui Hurst (b); Clive Nichols (tr). **100-101 GAP Photos:** John Glover (t); Joanna Kossak (b). **102-103 Farringford Estate:** E Penstone-Smith. **104 Jonathan Buckley:** (tl, tr). **104-105 Alamy Stock Photo:** The National Trust Photolibrary / Jonathan Buckle (b). **106-107 GAP Photos:** Carole Drake (t). **Jason Ingram:** (b). **108 GAP Photos:** Mark Bolton (t); Crole Drake (b). **110-111 Jason Ingram**. **112-113 Richard Bloom:** (t). **112 GAP Photos:** Richard Bloom (b). **113 Jason Ingram:** (b). **115 GAP Photos:** Charles Hawes (r). **Jason Ingram:** (l). **116-117 Alamy Stock Photo:** the red house image library. **118-119 RHS:** Jason Ingram. **120-121 RHS:** Mark Bolton (t). **GAP Photos:** Nicola Stocken (b). **121 RHS:** Mark Bolton (br). **122-123 Marianne Majerus Garden Images:** Marianne Majerus. **124-125 Richard Bloom**. **126 Alamy Stock Photo:** Will Perrett (t). **126-127 Andrew Merron:** (b). **128-129 Trebah Garden**. **131 Alamy Stock Photo:** Kevin Britland (tl). **Richard Bloom:** (b). **GAP Photos:** Carole Drake (tr). **132-133 Alamy Stock Photo:** mauritius image GmbH (t); The

National Trust Photolibrary (b). **134-135 Clive Nichols**. **136 Clive Nichols**. **137 Alamy Stock Photo:** Alison Thompson (r). **Jason Ingram:** (l). **141 GAP Photos:** Carole Drake (b). **Getty Images:** R A Kearton (t). **142-143 Richard Bloom**. **144-145 Richard Bloom:** (t). **145 Richard Bloom:** (b). **146-147 Alamy Stock Photo:** The National Trust Photolibrary. **148 Alamy Stock Photo:** The National Trust Photolibrary (t). **148-149 Alamy Stock Photo:** gardenpics (b). **149 Alamy Stock Photo:** Paul Quayle (t). **151 GAP Photos:** Charles Hawes (t, b). **152-153 Alamy Stock Photo:** Nigel McCall. **153 Alamy Stock Photo:** Alex Ramsay (r). **155 Alamy Stock Photo:** imageBROKER.com (tl); Derek Phillips (tr); Simon Whaley Landscapes (b). **156-157 Claire Takacs:** (t). **160 Ray Cox:** (l). **161 Ray Cox:** (r). **162-163 Ray Cox**. **164 Alamy Stock Photo:** John Potter (l). **164-165 Ray Cox:** (t, b). **166 Ray Cox:** (t, b). **166-167 Ray Cox**. **168-169 Ray Cox:** (b). **169 Ray Cox:** (tl, tr). **170 Ray Cox:** (tl, tr). **GAP Photos:** Carole Drake (b). **173 Ray Cox:** (t, b). **175 Ray Cox:** (t, b). **177 Ray Cox:** (tl, tr, b). **178 Ray Cox:** (l, r). **180-181 Ray Cox**. **182 Ray Cox:** (l, r). **183 Ray Cox**. **185 Ray Cox:** (tl, tr, b). **186 Ray Cox:** (l). **186-187 Ray Cox**. **188-189 Ray Cox**. **190 Ray Cox:** (tl). **190-191 Ray Cox:** (t, b). **192-193 Ray Cox**. **194-195 Alamy Stock Photo:** SW1. **198-199 Alamy Stock Photo:** The National Trust Photoblibrary / Andrew Butler. **200-201 Alamy Stock Photo:** The National Trust Photoblibrary / Andrew Butler (t). **201 Alamy Stock Photo:** The National Trust Photoblibrary / Andrew Butler (tr, b). **202 Alamy Stock Photo:** Design Pics Inc. (tr). **GAP Photos:** Tim Gainey (tl). **202-203 Jonathan Hession**. **204-205 Alamy Stock Photo:** George Munday (t); David Nixon (b). **207 Cluain na dTor:** Sarah Sayers (tl, tr). **Garden Exposures Photo Library:** Andrea Jones (b). **208-209 Jonathan Hession**. **211 Jonathan Hession:** (t). **Kylemore Abbey and Gardens Ltd.** (b). **212-213 Jonathan Hession**. **215 Richard Johnston:** (tr). **Richard Murphy:** (tl, b). **216-217 Jason Ingram**. **218 Marianne Majerus Garden Images:** Marianne Majerus (l, r). **219 Marianne Majerus Garden Images:** Marianne Majeru. **220-221 Marianne Majerus Garden Images:** Marianne Majerus. **222-223 Jonathan Hession**. **224-225 Airfield Estate:** Jonathan Hession (b). **225 Jonathan Hession:** (t). **226 Alamy Stock Photo:** Dawid Kalisinski (t). **227 Alamy Stock Photo:** Neil Machlachlan (b). **228-229 GAP Photos:** Lynn Keddie (b). **Jonathan Hession:** (t). **231 Jonathan Hession**. **232-233 Jonathan Hession:** (t, b). **233 Jonathan Hession:** (br). **234-235 Richard Murphy**. **234 Richard Murphy:** (l). **236-237 Clive Nichols**. **238-239 Jonathan Hession:** (t, b). **240-241 Alamy Stock Photo:** Bob Jenkin (t). **Getty Images:** Robin Bush (b). **243 Alamy Stock Photo:** RBlaser Photos (r); Chris Dorne (l). **244-245 Alamy Stock Photo:** scenicireland.com / Christopher Hall Photographic. **246-247 Alamy Stock Photo:** Johannes Rigg.

Cover image: Richard Bloom; image shows The Bressingham Gardens.

About the Authors

James Alexander-Sinclair FSGD is one of the foremost garden designers in the UK. He has designed gardens from Cornwall to the Western Isles and from London to Moscow. He is also an award-winning writer and served ten years as a member of the Council of the Royal Horticultural Society. He is an RHS Vice-President and received the Veitch Memorial Medal for outstanding contribution to horticulture in 2022. He is the RHS Ambassador for Garden Design and a Fellow of the Society of Garden Designers.

Matthew Biggs is a Kew-trained gardener, writer, and broadcaster, best known as a panellist on BBC Radio 4's *Gardeners' Question Time*. He is widely travelled, both in Britain and around the globe, visiting gardens and studying plants, and has contributed to books on garden history and the garden in art.

Phil Clayton is an author, gardener, and plantsman who writes about gardens, nurseries, and plants for a wide range of publications; his most recent books include *A Plant for Every Day of the Year* and *Parched*. He was named Roy Lancaster Features Writer of the Year by the Garden Media Guild in 2024.

Fionnuala Fallon is a National Botanic Gardens-trained horticulturist, author, garden writer and flower farmer-florist. She has been the gardening columnist for *The Irish Times* since 2011 and has also written features for *The English Garden* and *Gardens Illustrated*.

Antoinette Galbraith is a garden writer who lives, works, and tends to her garden in the Scottish Borders. She is a regular contributor to the magazines *Scottish Field* and *The English Garden*.

Annie Gatti is an Irish writer and editor, based in Somerset. She is co-author of *RHS Your Wellbeing Garden* and associate editor of *The Good Gardens Guide*. She was gardening editor of *Weekend, The Times*, re-launch editor of the *Garden Design Journal* and won the Garden Media Guild's Environmental Award in 2011.

David Hurrion has been growing plants and visiting gardens for more than 50 years. His wide knowledge and practical experience of garden history, design, and plants is based on a thorough botanical and scientific training, complemented by an in-depth knowledge of wildlife, geology, and climatology. David is the author of a number of books, most notably *The Raised Bed Book*. He lives with his partner, dog, and garden in Dorset.

Tony Russell has worked in horticulture for over 35 years, including 14 years in charge of Britain's National Arboretum at Westonbirt and 10 years as plant consultant to the National Trust. He has also presented several TV and radio programmes, as well as appearing as a panellist on BBC Radio 4's *Gardeners' Question Time*. Tony is the author of over 20 books on gardens, plants, and trees and is the editor of the annual publication *Great Gardens to Visit*.

Tamsin Westhorpe gardens at her family garden Stockton Bury in Herefordshire. She is an author, RHS Judge and speaker at home and abroad. Her career started with time spent as a park gardener and she later went on to become a college lecturer and editor of *The English Garden* magazine.

Senior Editor Alastair Laing
Senior Designer Glenda Fisher
Jacket Designer Maxine Pedliham
Editorial Assistant Athena Stacy
Publishing Assistant Emily Cannings
Senior Production Editor Tony Phipps
Senior Production Controller Stephanie McConnell
Editorial Director Ruth O'Rourke
Art Director Maxine Pedliham
Publishing Director Stephanie Jackson

Editorial Holly Kyte
Design Paul Reid
Picture Research Emily Hedges
Cartography James Macdonald

FOR THE RHS
Editor Simon Maughan
RHS Books Publisher Helen Griffin
Head of Editorial Tom Howard

First published in Great Britain in 2025 by
Dorling Kindersley Limited
20 Vauxhall Bridge Road,
London SW1V 2SA

The authorised representative in the EEA is
Dorling Kindersley Verlag GmbH. Arnulfstr. 124,
80636 Munich, Germany

Copyright © 2025 Dorling Kindersley Limited
A Penguin Random House Company
10 9 8 7 6 5 4 3 2 1
001-345498-Aug/2025

All rights reserved.

No part of this publication may be reproduced, stored in or introduced into a retrieval system, or transmitted, in any form, or by any means (electronic, mechanical, photocopying, recording, or otherwise), without the prior written permission of the copyright owner.

DK values and supports copyright. Thank you for respecting intellectual property laws by not reproducing, scanning or distributing any part of this publication by any means without permission. By purchasing an authorised edition, you are supporting writers and artists and enabling DK to continue to publish books that inform and inspire readers. No part of this publication may be used or reproduced in any manner for the purpose of training artificial intelligence technologies or systems. In accordance with Article 4(3) of the DSM Directive 2019/790, DK expressly reserves this work from the text and data mining exception.

A CIP catalogue record for this book
is available from the British Library.
ISBN: 978-0-2417-2260-2

Printed and bound in China

www.dk.com

This book was made with Forest Stewardship Council™ certified paper – one small step in DK's commitment to a sustainable future.
Learn more at www.dk.com/uk/information/sustainability